GALILEO GALILEI
1564–1642 •
Discovered law of pendulum motion

CAROLUS LINNAEUS
• 1707–1778
Classified the plant
and animal kingdoms

SIGMUND FREUD
• 1856–1939
Started psychoanalysis

GREGOR JOHANN MENDEL
1822–1884 •
Discovered principles of heredity

BARON ERNEST RUTHERFORD
1871–1937 •
Contributed to knowledge of
radioactivity and atomic structure

GUGLIELMO MARCONI
• 1874–1937
Invented the wireless telegraph

LOUIS AGASSIZ
• 1807–1873
Investigated glacial motion
and marine life

MICHAEL FARADAY
1791–1867 •
Discovered electromagnetic induction

SIR ISAAC NEWTON
• 1642–1727
Discovered laws of light,
gravity, motion and color

ALBERT EINSTEIN
1879–1955 •
Conceived the Theory of Relativity

WILHELM KONRAD ROENTGEN
• 1845–1923
Discovered X-rays

ALEXANDER GRAHAM BELL
1847–1922 •
Invented
the telephone

JOSEPH LISTER
• 1827–1912
Started antiseptic surgery

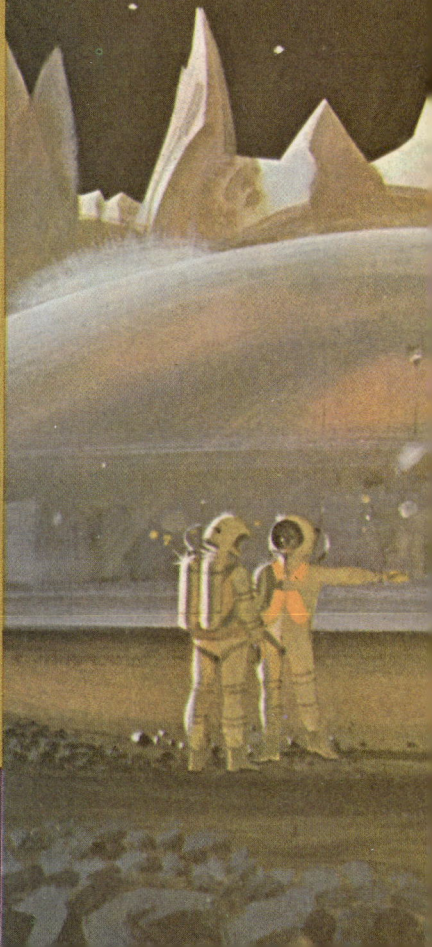

# YOUNG PEOPLE'S
# SCIENCE
## ENCYCLOPEDIA

*Edited by the Staff of*

### NATIONAL COLLEGE OF EDUCATION, Evanston, Ill.

#### ASSOCIATE EDITORS

HELEN J. CHALLAND, B.E., M.A., PH.D.
Chairman, Science Department, National
College of Education

DONALD A. BOYER, B.S., M.S., PH.D.
Science Education Consultant, Winnetka
Public Schools, Winnetka, Ill., Science,
National College of Education

W. RAY RUCKER, B.A., M.A., ED.D.
Former Dean of the College, National College of Education

#### EDITORIAL CONSULTANTS

ON THE STAFF OF NATIONAL COLLEGE OF EDUCATION

Elizabeth R. Brandt, B.A., M.Ed.

Eugene B. Cantelupe, B.A., M.F.A., Ph.D.

John H. Daugherty, B.S., M.A.

Irwin K. Feinstein, B.S., M.A., Ph.D.

Mary Gallagher, A.B., M.A., Ph.D.

Beatrice B. Garber, A.B., M.S., Ph.D.

Robert R. Kidder, A.B., M.A., Ph.D.

Jean C. Kraft, B.S., M.A., Ph.D.

Elise P. Lerman, B.A., B.F.A., M.F.A.

Mary-Louise Neumann, A.B., B.S. in L.S.

Lavon Rasco, B.A., M.A., Ph.D.

#### SPECIAL SUBJECT AREA CONSULTANTS

Krafft A. Ehricke, B.A.E., H.L.D.

Charles B. Johnson, B.S., M.A., M.S.

Raymond J. Johnson, B.B.A., Senior
Certificate in Industrial Engineering

Norma R. Rucker, B.S.

H. Kenneth Scatliff, M.D.

Ray C. Soliday, B.A., B.S., M.A.
(Deceased)

Fred R. Wilkin, Jr., B.S., M.Ed.

#### THE STAFF

| | | |
|---|---|---|
| PROJECT DIRECTOR | · | WALLACE B. BLACK |
| COORDINATING EDITOR | · | JEAN F. BLASHFIELD |
| ART DIRECTOR | · | BEN ROSEN |
| PHOTO AND ART EDITOR | · | MARTHA O'ROURKE |
| PRODUCTION EDITOR | · | ORLANDO T. CURCIO |

# YOUNG PEOPLE'S
# SCIENCE
# ENCYCLOPEDIA

*Edited by the Staff of*

## NATIONAL COLLEGE OF EDUCATION
### Evanston, Illinois

## VOLUME 4
# BR-CL

CHILDRENS PRESS, INC., CHICAGO 7

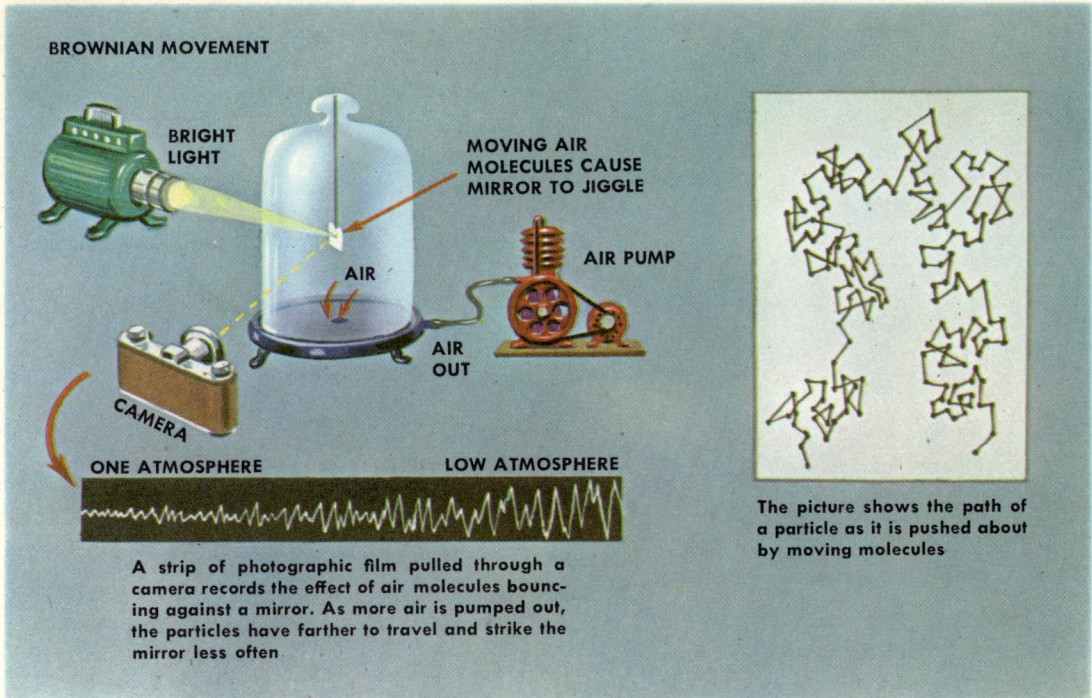

BROWNIAN MOVEMENT

BRIGHT LIGHT

MOVING AIR MOLECULES CAUSE MIRROR TO JIGGLE

AIR

AIR PUMP

AIR OUT

CAMERA

ONE ATMOSPHERE       LOW ATMOSPHERE

A strip of photographic film pulled through a camera records the effect of air molecules bouncing against a mirror. As more air is pumped out, the particles have farther to travel and strike the mirror less often

The picture shows the path of a particle as it is pushed about by moving molecules

**Brownian movement** The Brownian movement shows by experiment that small particles of matter (molecules) are in constant motion. When, in 1827, Robert Brown, an Englishman, put very fine powder in water, the particles moved around as though alive. He looked at them through his microscope. This movement was caused by water molecules constantly moving about and hitting the powder particles. The same thing happens to dust in the air when air molecules keep striking the tiny dust particles.

Robert Brown was born in Scotland in 1773. He was a famous botanist. In 1828 he published a paper on the general existence of active molecules in organic and inorganic substances. The real significance of his discovery was not appreciated until 50 years later. His experiments helped confirm the KINETIC THEORY of matter. According to this theory, all molecules are in constant motion except at ABSOLUTE ZERO which is the coldest anything can get.

The molecules of water or gases are too small to be seen directly, but placing very

small, insoluble dust or flour-like particles in a liquid permits the motion of liquid molecules to set the dust in motion. Usually, a microscope is used to observe the motion.

The Brownian movement may be observed in air without a microscope. On a sunny day, if an old window shade is pulled down, some rays of light will come through pin-hole cracks in the shade. In the semi-darkened room, dust, moving about at random, can be seen in the beam of light. This movement is not caused by air currents, but by the movement of air molecules. When enough air molecules bombard dust particles, the particles are set in motion. This shows how indirect evidence may be used in science to support a theory about the nature of matter.       J. H. D.

SEE ALSO: MOLECULAR THEORY

**Brussels sprouts** see Cabbage

**Bryophytes** (BRY-uh-fights) Bryophytes are the group, or *phylum,* of plants that include the true mosses and the liverworts. They are very old plants and are simple when compared with some of the more developed plants. Bryophytes do not have true roots, stems, or leaves. They get their

**Hornworts are small, lobed plants**

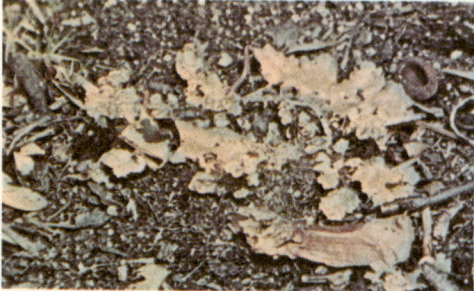

Courtesy Society For Visual Education, Inc.
**Liverworts are the simplest bryophytes**

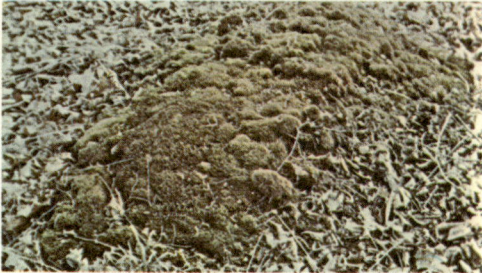

Courtesy Society For Visual Education, Inc.
**Mosses are the best known bryophytes**

water through a thread of cells, called a *rhizoid*. The rhizoid also acts as an anchor and holds the plant in place.

Most bryophytes grow in moist places on the soil, on rotting logs, or on the bark of living trees. A few bryophytes live in dry places and some are aquatic, or live in fresh water. In the warm, damp tropics much of the thick vegetation that hangs from tree branches belongs to the bryophyte phylum. Bryophyte species are also found in the tundras of Arctica.

There are 3 different groups of bryophytes: the liverworts, the hornworts, and the mosses. The LIVERWORTS are the simplest and are flat, ribbonlike, green plants. There are about 9,000 different species or kinds of liverworts. The hornworts are small, green plants that have lobes and many rhizoids. The mosses are probably the best known of the entire group. While liverworts are not apt to be noticed on river banks, mosses cover wide areas along streams, and are

usually seen on the rocks and trees or in the water. There are about 14,000 different species of mosses.

Although the bryophytes are simple plants, their method of reproducing is not simple. One generation of the plant reproduces by forming cells called spores. These spores will develop into the second generation. This second generation produces male and female cells (gametes) which unite to form new plants. This process is called ALTERNATION OF GENERATIONS.

J. D. B.

SEE ALSO: MOSS, SPORE FORMATION

**B.T.U.** see British Thermal Unit

**Bubonic plague**    (boo-BAHN-ick) Bubonic plague derives its name from the change which it causes in the human body and from the fact that it tends to strike large numbers of the population at one time. *Bubonic* means a swelling of certain glands in the body. The disease is very contagious.

The disease is spread by a flea which has been living on an infected rat. The cause of the disease is a short, rod-shaped bacterium with rounded ends called the *Bacillus pestis*. When a person becomes infected, a painful swelling of the glands is found in the groin, armpit, neck, or even inside the chest, in which case PNEUMONIA develops. These rounded swellings vary from the size of a walnut to that of a goose egg. They can become so swollen that they burst and become open sores. Black and blue spots sometimes found on the body gave rise, in the early days, to the term *Black Death*. Actually these spots marked the bite of the flea carrying the disease from rat to man.

The victim of bubonic plague is very sick. He develops a high temperature in the first, second or third days. The death rate is high, especially at the height of an epidemic. Prevention is a community problem. Exterminate the rats!

The use of the newly developed ANTIBIOTICS has cut down the death rate from this disease. For explorers and others who travel in countries where the disease is present, a vaccine made from cultures of the germ has been developed.                    H. K. S.

SEE ALSO: BLACK DEATH

Courtesy Society For Visual Education, Inc.
**Leaf buds will form new stems and branches**

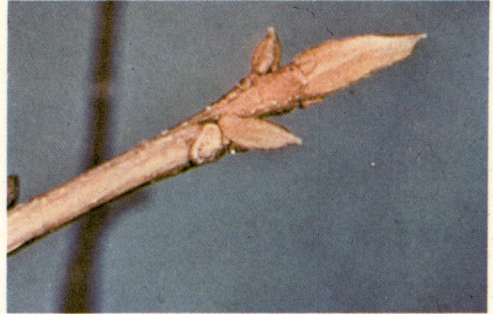
**Buckeye tree**

**Buckeye** The buckeye is a tree native to the United States. It has beautifully shaped leaves which spread out like a fan from a central point. These are dark green in color.

The buckeye tree bears a round-shaped, shiny brown fruit which people do not eat. However, it is eaten by some members of the rodent family. For many years, there was a superstition that if one carried a buckeye in his pocket, he would not have the disease arthritis.

Eastern buckeyes have yellow or pink flowers that grow in loose clusters. The California species has a smooth, pear-shaped fruit and white flowers.    V. V. N.

**Buckwheat** Buckwheat is a green, leafy plant. Its three-sided seeds are ground to make a flour often used in pancakes. It is not related to WHEAT or to other grains which belong to the grass family.

Buckwheat grows to be about three feet high and has heart-shaped leaves. Bees like its small, sweet-smelling flowers and make a dark, strong-tasting honey from its nectar.

Buckwheat is used as a "first crop" on newly cleared land and is planted to be plowed under in order to improve the soil. It can be grown on ground too wet for other grains and is often planted to kill weeds by shading and smothering them. Buckwheat hulls and straw make fine mulches.  J. M. C.

**Buckwheat**

**Bud** Buds are growths on stems and contain tiny leaves or flowers. They are protected by scales. They may be active (growing) or dormant (resting before growth). Buds can best be observed by collecting twigs of trees or shrubs. By placing these in water in a warm place during the early spring, their regular spring growth can be watched.

A lengthwise cut through a winter bud will show the growing tip of the stem, the young leaves and the hard outer scales. These scales may be coated with RESIN or with short, dense hairs. They serve to protect the inner parts from drought.

The *terminal* bud at the tip of the stem is responsible for elongation of the stem. A hormone is produced by this bud which causes the central stem to become a suppressor growth of the lateral buds lower down on the stem. This is most striking in firs and spruces which show a strong central stem.

Buds may be located alternately on the stem, or they may be opposite each other. In either case their position on the stem marks the *node*. The space between adjacent buds is the *internode*.

Buds develop in the *leaf axils* (angles where the stem of a leaf joins a branch). Even after the leaf has fallen, a scar remains just below the bud.

As buds become active in the spring, the stem between the young leaves elongates considerably. However, the stem between the bud scales grows very little. For this reason, the fallen scales leave a distinct ring around the twig which marks the beginning of each year's growth. The age of a young twig may be determined by counting the number of rings.

**Fig. I— LONGITUDINAL SECTION THROUGH TERMINAL BUD OF A WOODY PLANT**
a. SHOOT APEX
b. EMBRYONIC LEAVES
c. BUD SCALES

**Fig. II— DORMANT STEM WITH BUDS**
a. TERMINAL BUD
b. LATERAL (AXILLARY) BUD
c. LEAF SCAR
d. NODE
e. INTERNODE

**Fig. III— THREE-YEAR-OLD TWIG SHOWING ANNUAL RINGS LEFT BY TERMINAL BUD**

Buds vary greatly in appearance from the eyes of the POTATO tuber, which are really *lateral* buds, to the familiar CABBAGE head, which is a *terminal* bud.

In addition to producing stems, leaves, and flowers, buds develop growth substances which affect the whole plant.     M. D. F.
SEE ALSO: BOTANY, BULBS, PLANT

**Budding** see Reproduction, asexual

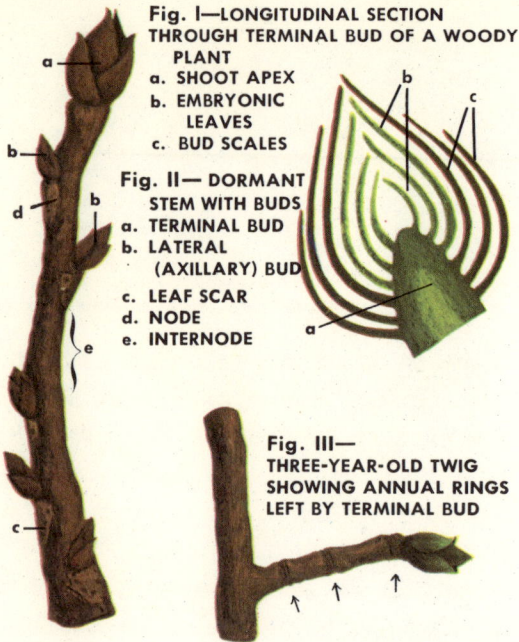

**Buffalo** Buffaloes are large wild OXEN with long horns. The water buffalo of India and the Cape buffalo of Africa are true members of the buffalo family. The American buffalo is a *bison,* not a true buffalo. It has a large brown body about eleven feet long, and weighs from 900 to 3000 pounds. Its huge head, front legs and high-humped shoulders are covered with long shaggy hair. The horns on its head are short and curved. About one hundred years ago these large mammals roamed in great herds over the western plains of the United States.

Historians believe that there were about sixty million buffalo (bison) in America before the white man came. They lived in enormous herds, some over ten miles wide. When they ran, the sound of their hoofs was like thunder. In spring and fall the huge herds would travel (migrate) as far as 400 miles to find good feeding grounds. They wore trails over grasslands and mountains that were later used by engineers in laying out modern roads and railroads.

The early Plains Indians depended on the bison for food, shelter, and clothing. They killed only as many buffalo as they needed, and they used every part of each animal— flesh, hide, bones, teeth, etc. However, as the white man moved west over the prairies he slaughtered millions of bison for their hides alone.

In 1850 there were about twenty million bison on the plains. In 1889 only 550 were left. It was then that efforts were made to save the American buffalo. Game laws were passed and conservation areas were created.

The American buffalo belongs to the same animal family (BOVIDAE) as cattle, sheep, and goats. It feeds on grasses and small plants.

One baby (calf) is born to the mother bison (cow) in late spring. It stays with its mother for one year.     D. J. A.
SEE ALSO: UNGULATA

**Water buffalo of Indo-China**
Chicago Natural History Museum

**American bison**
Chicago Natural History Museum

**Bugs** All insects are not bugs, but all bugs are insects. There are over twenty groups of insects, and the true bugs make up only one of these groups. Bugs' wings are thick at the base near the body but thin and delicate at the ends. There may be a diamond-shaped pattern on the thorax. These are the easiest things to look for in telling bugs from all the other insects.

Bugs range in size from a fraction of an inch to four inches. They have sucking mouth parts with sharp beaks. They have a pair of compound eyes and often two simple eyes. They develop gradually from egg to nymph to adult. This is called *incomplete* METAMORPHOSIS. Bugs live on land, in the water, or on plants and other animals. They can make sounds by rubbing their legs and wings against other parts of their bodies.

The *aquatic bugs* live in ponds and streams, while a few are marine. They are *predaceous,* which means they attack other insects, snails, and small fish. The *water striders* take advantage of the SURFACE TENSION of the water to keep them afloat. They travel at a remarkable pace. The *back-swimmers* do just that—swim on their back, but they can also fly. Their backs resemble the bottom of a boat, and their third pair of legs serves as paddles. The *water boatmen* swim about in a crazy fashion. They eat algae and diatoms. In turn, the Mexican Indians eat them. The *giant waterbugs* are so large that they will readily attack frogs, salamanders, and fish four times larger than themselves. Their bites may cause rather painful swelling. They are called *electric-light bugs* since they are attracted to light. They hibernate in the adult stage.

The *stinkbugs* have two glands on the thorax which give off an unpleasant odor. However, birds are not bothered by this and do not hesitate to consume stink bugs in great quantities. These bugs are green or brown. They suck plant juices and are destructive to garden crops. The *harlequin* (meaning "clown") is a gaily colored bug

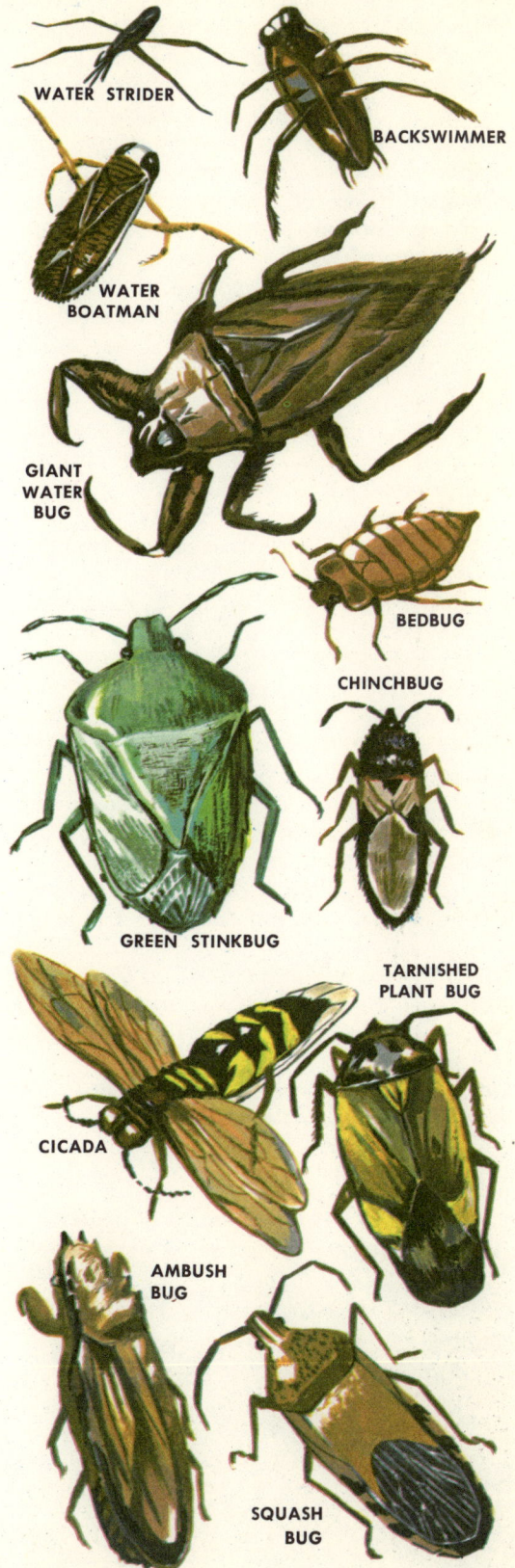

WATER STRIDER

BACKSWIMMER

WATER BOATMAN

GIANT WATER BUG

BEDBUG

CHINCHBUG

GREEN STINKBUG

TARNISHED PLANT BUG

CICADA

AMBUSH BUG

SQUASH BUG

that is a pest because it destroys garden plants such as radishes, turnips, and cabbage.

*Bedbugs* feed on birds and mammals. They have nocturnal feeding habits, sneaking out of crevices in homes and attacking their prey. The eggs of these bugs take two months to develop into adults. Since a pair may have three or four generations each year, they continue to be pests once a place is infested with them.

One species of *cicadas* takes seventeen years to complete the life cycle. In spring and early summer the female bores holes in the bark of trees and lays eggs. In six weeks the nymph hatches, drops to the ground, and burrows in. It feeds on the juices of roots and finally appears as an adult seventeen years later.

The *chinch bugs* were brought to America from the tropics. Since their natural enemies were left behind, they have become real pests. They overrun grain fields, destroying millions of dollars worth of grain annually. The nymphs are red and the adults are gray and brown. The female lays 500 eggs two or three times per year.

APHIDS (plant lice) and scale insects are a large group of wingless bugs. They attack many plants, especially the citrus and other fruit trees. The *ambush bugs* are known for their bizarre forms and feeding habits. They jump from their hiding place and grab their victims with mouthparts that tear and suck. The *squashbugs* have a strong, offensive odor. They feed on melons, gourds, and pumpkins.

There are 55,000 species of true bugs. Not everything that crawls is a "bug." The ladybug, June bug, and lightning bug, for example, are BEETLES and not true bugs.

H. J. C.

SEE ALSO: INSECTA

**A kind of milkweed bug, plant louse**
Buchsbaum

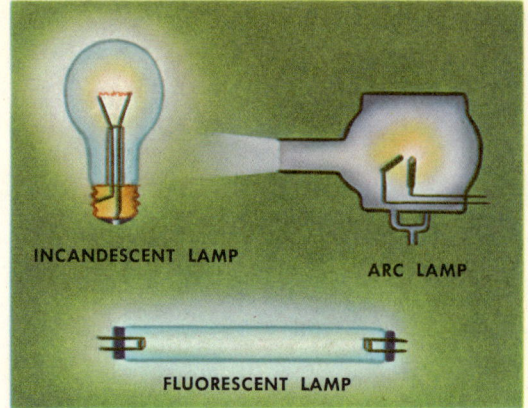

INCANDESCENT LAMP      ARC LAMP

FLUORESCENT LAMP

**Bulb, electric** An electric light bulb is a lamp which produces visible and invisible light by means of an electric current passing through its circuit. Electric lights may be classified as one of three types: 1) arc lamp, 2) incandescent lamp, and 3) vapor lamp.

### ARC LAMP

Two carbon ELECTRODES with a small space or gap between them form the light-producing portion of the electrical circuit. When a current flows, an electric arc flashes in the gap and produces a brilliant white light. The arc lamp was rapidly replaced with the incandescent lamp as the latter became more dependable.

### INCANDESCENT LAMP

This lamp is commonly called "the electric light bulb." It consists of three main parts: (a) the glass bulb or envelope, (b) the filament, and (c) the base. The bulb contains the metal filament (a fine wire) in a VACUUM or inert gas. The base seals the bulb and provides a means of passing the electric current through the filament. As the current flows, the filament becomes heated and produces light. The vacuum or inert gas enables the filament to glow more intensely than it would in ordinary air. Although the incandescent lamp which used a platinum wire and glass tube was invented in the early 19th century, it was not until 1879 that THOMAS EDISON produced the first practical lamp. His lamp consisted of a carbonized cotton thread for a filament which was operated in a high vacuum. In 1880, Joseph Wilson Swan developed the hermetically-sealed (air-tight) enclosure which is now used.

**TURNING ELECTRICAL ENERGY
INTO LIGHT ENERGY**

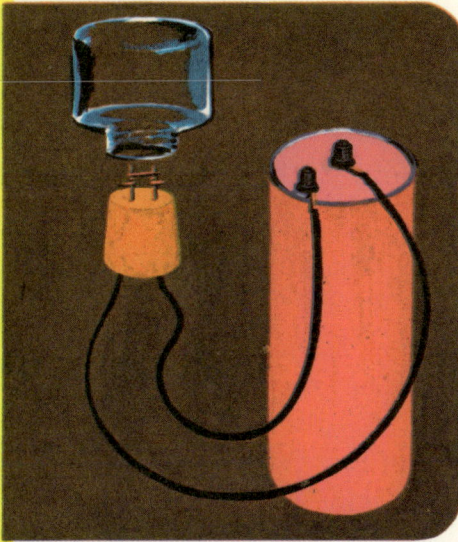

1  Push two exposed ends of bell wire through a cork. Wrap fine wire around the end of one wire, then across and around the second wire. This will be the filament in a home-made light bulb.
2  Insert the cork into the mouth of an ink bottle. Connect the other ends of the wire to a series of dry cells.
3  When the circuit is complete the filament will glow. Eventually the filament burns up since there is oxygen in the bottle. The oxygen has been removed in commercial bulbs.

Filament materials constantly were improved as they were changed from carbonized cotton and paper to bamboo to cellulose to metallized carbon. In 1907, the first TUNGSTEN filament lamp was marketed. Because tungsten was so fragile, a method of making it ductile had to be developed. Inert gases retard filament oxidation and, therefore, replaced the vacuum. By coiling the filament, the light efficiency was improved even more.

### VAPOR LAMP

The vapor lamp may appear similar to the incandescent lamp or may have the shape of a long thin tube with bases on each end. The tube type is known as the *fluorescent lamp*. This lamp has tungsten filaments at each base which serve as electrodes. The tube, coated on the inside with fluorescent material, contains current-conducting gas. When a high voltage is applied the current starts to flow from one electrode to the other. Ultraviolet rays formed by the current flow excite the fluorescent coating and make it glow. A high voltage is needed to start the current. Thereafter, the normal voltage of 120 volts is enough to maintain the current flow. A device called a "starter" provides the initial high voltage. Vapor lamps are more efficient than incandescent lamps. Fluorescent lamps range from 30-65 lumens per watt.

Mercury and sodium lamps are two types of high-intensity vapor lamps which operate very efficiently, with approximately 55 lumens per watt. A third electrode is used in the mercury lamp to start the current flow. The globe contains argon gas and a small amount of mercury.

The sodium lamp is built like a vacuum bottle since it has a double-walled envelope. Two sets of electrodes are used to conduct current through the metallic sodium and neon gas contents. The sodium vapor lamp produces a yellow light making it more desirable for outdoor than indoor use.    E. I. D.
SEE ALSO: ARC, LIGHT

Edison's original bulb had sewing thread as the filament. It burned for about forty hours

The presence of sugar and starch in a bulb can be easily tested. One-fourth teaspoon juice from a bulb is placed in a test tube containing one tablespoon of Benedict's solution. After being heated in a water bath, the liquid will turn orange if sugar is present. For the starch test, a portion of a bulb is crushed into a tablespoon of water. A few drops of iodine will turn the liquid purple if starch is present

**Bulbs** Bulbs are much like BUDS with roots. A bulb is a flattened disc-like stem from which many fleshy, scale-like leaves arise. The bottom of the bulb bears ROOTS. The main function of a bulb is to store foods such as starches and sugars for the plant.

Many flowers such as daffodils, hyacinths, and tulips grow from bulbs. The stored food is used to produce flowers and leaves. Leaves continue to process food which is stored in the bulb and used for next year's growth. The most familiar bulb is the ONION which is rich in sugar and is widely used for food.                M. D. F.
SEE ALSO: CHLOROPHYLL, PHOTOSYNTHESIS

**Bullet** see Projectiles, Weapons

**Bullhead** Bullhead is the name for several species of CATFISH. The commonest one is the brown bullhead or horned pout, which ranges in size from 12-18 inches. It is a scavenger.

**BUNSEN BURNER**
FLAME COLOR VARIES WITH AMOUNT OF AIR IN THE GASEOUS MIXTURE

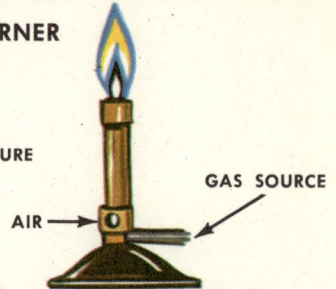

AIR → | GAS SOURCE

**Bunsen burner** The Bunsen burner is a gas burner giving a very hot flame. It is widely used in school science laboratories. The burner consists of a metal tube on a base connected with a rubber tube to the gas supply. Small openings near the bottom permit air to mix with gas. The flame is pale blue. Gas stove burners work the same way.

If insufficient air is mixed with the gas, the Bunsen flame burns with a yellow light. The yellow flame is cooler and produces soot. This soot is really carbon particles that are not completely oxidized to the hotter, blue CARBON DIOXIDE seen in properly mixed flames of air and gas.          J. H. D.

**Bunting** (BUN-ting) Buntings are small birds living in shrubs and cut-over forests. The young and females are brownish-gray, but the males are brightly colored. Three of the four kinds found in the United States are blue. The *indigo* is completely blue, the GROSBEAK has chestnut wing bars, while the *lazuli* has white wing bars with a chestnut breast. The *painted bunting* is mixed red, green and blue.

**Painted bunting**

Lighted buoy

**Buoy** A buoy is an anchored, floating object which marks channels or danger spots in a body of water. It may contain bells or lights as additional warning signals.
SEE: BUOYANCY

**Buoyancy** Buoyancy is that force which allows objects to float in liquids and in the air. When a swimmer floats on his back in the water he is using the law of buoyancy. When a BALLOON floats in the air for a period of time this is also buoyancy.

Buoyancy is an upward force pushing on an object that is floating or submerged in a gas or liquid. This force is opposite in direction from the downward force due to the weight of the object. Also, this upward force is equal to the weight of the liquid or gas displaced by the object. Both these forces arise through the action of GRAVITY.

That law of science which covers buoyancy is called *Archimedes' principle* and is stated as follows: "An object immersed in or floating on a liquid is buoyed up by a force equal to the weight of that liquid displaced by the object." For example, if a boy entered a bathtub full of water and he was able to float on top of it, the weight of the boy would be exactly equal to the weight of the water that overflowed when he got in.

Buoyancy explains why a boat can stay afloat on the water without sinking and why a SUBMARINE must carefully take on extra water in its tanks in order to submerge below the surface of the water. In order to float, the floating object must have a lower average DENSITY than the liquid which is holding it afloat. Since density means the weight of a material in a certain volume, one can easily understand how a cupful of iron would sink, while a cupful of cork would float in water. The iron is very much heavier per cupful than water and cork is lighter per cupful

✳ **THINGS TO DO**

**TESTING THE BUOYANCY OF A GAS**

1  Fasten a small cardboard carton to each end of a stick with a piece of string. Hold the stick in the center by a third string. Pour carbon tetrachloride into a deep pan or pail.

2  Hold one carton in the pan but do not let it touch the liquid. The carton will rise.

3  The carton containing air displaces a certain amount of carbon tetrachloride gas. Therefore, the carton is buoyed up by a force equal to the weight of the gas it has displaced.

than water. A stone will sink in water, but is buoyed up by a force equal to the weight of the water displaced. The weight of the stone is greater than the buoyancy force upward, so it sinks.

Buoyancy applies to lighter-than-air craft such as balloons and blimps and other AIRSHIPS. These floating objects are filled with gases such as helium which have a very low density and therefore give the balloons an overall lower density than the air surrounding it.                    M. S.
SEE ALSO: ARCHIMEDES

Luther Burbank

**Burbank, Luther** (1849–1926) Burbank was a famous American horticulturist who created many new vegetables, grains, fruits, flowers, and trees. He also improved such familiar plants as the potato and blackberry.

When he was a small boy, Burbank was interested in nature. In Lancaster, Massachusetts, where he was born, Burbank attended the town academy. He later worked in a factory, but was extremely unhappy, and eventually he became a market gardener. He also raised seeds.

In 1875 Burbank moved to California, where the results of his work changed the agricultural practices in that part of the country. He achieved his amazing results by cross-pollinating plants of the same species to make a stronger, better plant, and by uniting two different plants to produce a new species. To cross-pollinate, he placed the pollen from the ANTHER of one flower upon the STIGMA of the other, and then allowed the marvelous process of fertilization to take place. He always chose the best plants and rejected the poorest. He examined hundreds of thousands of plants in order to find the strongest. His patience was endless.

One of the most interesting of Burbank's new plants was the Shasta daisy, named after Mt. Shasta in California. It was bred from the English daisy, the wild American daisy, and the Japanese daisy. A most unusual and delicious new species of fruit was the plumcot, a combination of the Japanese plum and the apricot. The Primus berry, a combination of the California dewberry and the Siberian raspberry, was without doubt the most important new species, because it was the first recorded fixed species directly created by man. Perhaps Burbank named this berry *Primus* because *primus* is a Latin word meaning *first*.                    D. H. J.

SEE ALSO: HORTICULTURE, HYBRIDIZATION

**Burns** A burn is an injury caused by fire or heat of some kind. There are three main kinds of burns. A *first-degree burn* makes the skin red and sore. In a *second-degree burn,* blisters form on the skin. A *third-degree burn* destroys deeper tissues. Burns may be caused either by moist or dry heat, by electricity, by strong ACIDS, or by strong alkalies.

If the burn is severe and extensive, the greatest dangers are shock and infection. Therefore, anyone giving treatment should try to prevent shock and infection and relieve the pain as much as possible. Any good burn ointment can be applied to a minor burn, after which it should be covered with a loose, sterile bandage. A thick paste of bicarbonate of soda (baking soda), made by mixing a small amount of water with soda, will usually ease the sting. In a second degree burn, it is important to avoid breaking the blister.

For treatment of severe scalds or burns, a doctor should be called immediately. The patient should be treated for shock until the doctor arrives. A patient in shock should be laid on his back with the head lower than the feet, covered with blankets, and kept as quiet as possible.

Acid burns should first be washed thoroughly with clean water and then treated with the soda solution. Alkali burns may be treated similarly but with a weak vinegar solution. All chemical burns should be referred to a doctor for final treatment.

Sunburn should be treated as a regular burn. Mild cases may be relieved by applying olive oil, cold cream, or other lotions and creams. The best way to avoid sunburn is to limit exposure until the skin is used to the sun. If excessive exposure occurs, serious illness may result.                    V. V. N.
SEE ALSO: FIRST AID

**Burro** A burro is a small, strong, surefooted DONKEY. It can carry heavy loads for its size.

Spaniards brought these stubborn little donkeys to Mexico and America during the Spanish colonial days. The word "burro" is the Spanish word for donkey. They became so valuable to the Mexican Indians as pack

Burro

animals that many were kept as pets. Burros are still used in parts of Mexico to carry pottery, firewood and other heavy loads.

Burros were also valuable to the American prospectors hunting for gold in the desert. These little animals were able to endure great hardships and seemed to thrive out on the hot desert in spite of lack of water and vegetation.                    D. J. A.

**Burrow** A burrow is a tunnel or a hole dug in the ground by a small animal such as a badger, a chipmunk, or a fox. A burrow is used by the animal as a home or a hiding place.

**Bushmaster** see Snakes

**Buttercup** There are about twelve hundred different kinds of buttercups. Some grow wild. Many others are found blooming in flower gardens. They grow best in cooler parts of the North Temperate Zone.

Wild buttercups have glossy yellow flowers. The leaves have deep notches. They have a poisonous, acid juice.

Garden flowers belonging to the buttercup family may have symmetrically shaped flowers as do the PEONY, anemone, and love-in-a-mist. Others, such as columbine, monkshood and larkspur, bear flowers which are irregular or one-sided in shape.    I. H. S.
SEE ALSO: WILD FLOWERS

Bulb buttercup

**Butterflies** Some of the most beautiful animals in the world are butterflies. They have long slender bodies and two pairs of wings. There are several ways the insect hunter can tell a butterfly from a MOTH. The feelers (antennae) of the butterfly are thin with knobs on the ends. The moths' antennae are feathery. The butterfly flies in the daytime and, when resting, will fold its wings up like a sail of a boat. The moth usually flies at night and, when resting, spreads its wings like those of an airplane.

Butterflies go through a complete change from egg to adult. The female lays eggs on plants which will be the food for the young larvae. The LARVA is called a CATERPILLAR. It does not form a cocoon; instead the resting stage is a *chrysalis*. The insect is a chrysalis through winter, then it becomes an adult. Most butterflies produce one brood a year.

The adult butterfly has a sucking mouthpart and a long structure called a *proboscis*. With this device it is able to suck nectar from deep within the flower parts. Since butterflies' feeding habits take them from plant to plant, they are useful in cross-pollinating flowers. The caterpillar has a chewing mouthpart and will devour leaves of many varieties of plants. Some eat aphids (plant lice) which are injurious to many cultivated plants.

The distinctive color of the butterfly's wings may be due to one of two conditions. The PIGMENT may be embedded in the scales of the wings; or, the ridges on the scales are in such a position that they diffract the light rays, producing a metallic appearance. Some butterflies exhibit MIMICRY. The *viceroy* looks like the *monarch* except it is smaller. Since the monarch is distasteful to many birds, the viceroy is also avoided as a meal. Other butterflies depend upon PROTECTIVE COLORATION. When the wings of a *dead-leaf* butterfly are folded skyward, it resembles its name.

## WHAT BUTTERFLY WILL IT BE?

1   Collect caterpillars or the chrysalises of several species of butterflies. Note the leaves of the plants where they are found. This is their food.

2   Place them in a container and leave it outside through the winter months. If they are brought inside in the fall the adult butterfly will emerge around December when no food is available.

3   In the early spring transfer the chrysalis to an insect cage. Supply them with fresh leaves (each species prefers certain plants).

4   Set them free when the study and observation of their life cycle has been completed.

The orange sulphur feeds on clover

The black swallowtail is identified by the double row of yellow spots

All photos Courtesy Society For Visual Education, Inc.
The cosmopolite has scaly wings

The *swallowtail* butterflies are among the largest—the giant swallowtail has a wing spread from four to six inches. They have "tails" projecting from the end of the wings. The larvae give off a musky odor which protects them from being eaten. The caterpillars enjoy the leaves of garden plants like carrots and parsnips. Some will feast in citrus orchards. They remain nine days in a chrysalis, and the adults appear usually in beautiful black and yellow attire.

The *monarch,* or milkweed, butterfly is one of the most common and interesting butterflies in North America. The adult lays pale green eggs on the leaves of milkweed. The caterpillar has distinctive black and yellow stripes. It sheds its skin four times as it grows and molts. It is one of the few insects that migrates regularly. Monarchs leave their northern summer homes in large groups and will fly hundreds of miles to a southern habitat. They return one by one in the spring. It is not certain whether the ones returning north in the spring are the old adults or new young ones.

There are over 10,000 species in the U.S.A. and Canada, classified into many groups. The *fritillaries* comprise one of the largest groups. The caterpillars are spiny in appearance and feed at night on violets and goldenrod. The adults are distinguished by their much shortened front legs.

The group called *buckeyes* are so named because of the prominent eyespots on their wings. They have brown chrysalises, and the adults inhabit the open fields. On a beautiful summer day it is fun to try to identify these beautiful insects: the red admiral, the painted lady or thistle butterfly, the cabbage and alfalfa butterflies, the coppers, the blues, and the hairstreak varieties.     H. J. C.

SEE ALSO: INSECTA, METAMORPHOSIS

All photos Courtesy Society For Visual Education, Inc.
**The cabbage butterflies are common in the U.S.**

**Western swallowtail has a slim smooth body**

**The aphrodite fritillary, like all fritillaries, is a brush-footed butterfly**

**Pearl crescent**

**Meadow fritillary**

**Monarch butterflies migrate like birds**

**Admiral Richard E. Byrd**

**Byrd, Richard Evelyn** (1888–1957) Byrd was an American explorer, aviator, and naval officer. He was the first person to fly over both the North and South poles, and he did much to develop important devices and methods of navigation.

Born in Winchester, Virginia, on October 25, 1888, Richard E. Byrd attended the Virginia Military Academy and the University of Virginia. He then studied at the U.S. Naval Academy, graduating in 1912. Following graduation, he served four years in the navy and then entered aviation service.

In 1925 Byrd went on the first of his many expeditions. He served as flight commander with the MacMillan expedition to Greenland. For the first time planes were used in arctic exploration. The following year, on May 9, Byrd and Floyd Bennett flew to the North Pole and returned in fifteen and one-half hours. One year later, in July of 1927, Byrd, with another pilot and two navigators, attempted to fly across the Atlantic Ocean, but they were forced down at sea and rescued after a terrifying experience.

In 1928 Byrd organized a scientific expedition to ANTARCTICA. Accompanying him were thirty-two scientists, specialists in the fields of aerology, geography, geology, meteorology, physics, radio engineering, and topography. These specialists took with them the most elaborate equipment ever used in exploration. For Byrd's enormous contribution to science, the U.S. Congress bestowed on him the rank of rear admiral.

Between 1933 and 1935 Byrd conducted a scientific survey of the Antarctic continent. In 1939 he returned to explore 900 miles of coastline around Marie Byrd Land.

To acquaint others with his polar adventures, Byrd wrote *Alone, Skyward, Little America,* and *Discovery.*	D. H. J.

**Cabbage** Cabbage is a leafy plant which is eaten as a vegetable. It is made into a salad when shredded raw, or may be boiled, or pickled for sauerkraut. Cabbage heads look like huge buds growing on top of short stalks. The heads may be round, oblong, flat, or cone-shaped.

Cabbage seeds may be sown in flat boxes during February or March and kept in a cool room. The seedlings should be kept moist and transplanted as they grow larger. After the danger of frost is past, the cabbage plants can be set outside in the garden. Cabbage should be raised in well-drained soil, properly enriched with plant food. It takes about one hundred days for cabbage to mature. Late varieties of cabbage should be set out in the garden about August first.

Other varieties are red cabbage, savory, CAULIFLOWER, Brussels sprouts, broccoli, KOHLRABI, and kale. M. R. L.

**Cables** A cable is a length of heavy rope or covered wire. A nautical cable secures a boat to a dock. A mechanical cable pulls suspended cable cars through the air, holds suspension BRIDGES, and lifts elevators.

An electric cable, made of copper or lightweight aluminum, carries ELECTRICITY to light the houses in a town. A power cable, which is sometimes 200 or more miles long, carries power to factories and other places that use a lot of power.

By means of an electric current, a communications cable carries voices from city to city on TELEPHONE wires overhead on poles or underground in ducts. A submarine cable carries words by electrical signal from continent to continent across the bottom of an ocean.

Underground cables are used more and more to carry communication and power lines. The first long distance underground telephone cable was laid in 1902 between New York City and Newark, New Jersey. In 1942 an all-cable, underground telephone route that spanned the nation was completed.

*Submarine cables:* In 1843 Morse, inventor of the telegraph, suggested that a cable be laid under water between the United States and England. At that time messages could be sent across water only as fast as ships could carry them on a written page.

Attempts were made to lay a cable across the Atlantic. The cables broke in laying, or they failed to work after they were laid. On one attempt the British iron steamship Great Eastern, the largest ship then afloat, lost a thousand miles of cable at sea.

In 1866 CYRUS W. FIELD succeeded in laying a cable across the Atlantic Ocean after trying for eleven years. The cable connected Canada to Newfoundland and went across to Ireland. In 1902 a cable was laid across the Pacific Ocean from San Francisco to Honolulu. Today the whole world is connected with cables that carry messages at the speed of hundreds of words per minute. P. G. B.
SEE ALSO: MORSE, SAMUEL; TELEVISION

**Cacao** see Cocoa

A large telephone cable carries many fine wires within it

**Cactus** Cactus is the name for more than 1700 different plants. Some cacti are very large and tree-like. Other cacti are climbing vines. Still others look like tiny "balls." Most of these plants are alike because they have needle-like *spines* instead of leaves, soft-looking green bodies, and most live in hot dry places. Many cacti have large, pretty flowers which bloom in the spring. No cactus has blue flowers. While cacti grow in DESERTS all over the world today, they first grew only in the Americas.

Cactus flower         Saguaro, or giant cactus

All photos Courtesy Society For Visual Education, Inc.

**Barrel cactus. These cactus plants can be found in deserts of the Southwest**

Because the cactus lives in places where it very seldom rains, it stores great amounts of water in large cells in the center of the stem. The *barrel* cactus, which is common in the deserts of the United States, holds nine times its own weight in water. Many thirsty travelers drink from this cactus by cutting off the top, crushing the inside of the cactus between two stones, and then squeezing it in their hands. The *prickly pear* has a flat, fleshy, sectional stem on which yellow or reddish flowers bloom.

The cactus produces a juicy fruit inside of which are the seeds. The skin or peel of this fruit, like the green surface of the cactus itself, grows in such a way that it keeps the water inside. Instead of broad flat leaves such as other plants have, the cactus has hard narrow spines which do not dry out. The cactus is so completely fitted for living with very little water that too much rain can kill it.

While the body of the cactus, which is actually its *stem,* looks soft and fleshy, this is not usually the case. The *giant* cactus of the Southwest, which grows forty to fifty feet tall, has a material inside it that is so stiff that the Indians used it to make carrying poles and frames for papoose cradles. They also used the hollowed out trunk of the barrel cactus as a cooking pot.

The spines of the cactus serve a double usefulness. Not only do they prevent evaporation, but they protect the cactus from animals which would otherwise eat it. The roots of most cacti branch widely so that when the rain does fall, they are able to absorb a great deal of it.

Thus, the cactus is well adapted to its life in arid climates. The shallow network of roots efficiently catch the rain which the central stem tissue stores for use in the dry season. Its protecting spines have no pores (stomata), and the stem has fewer stomata than other plants. Even those it does have are often set in depressions as a further safeguard against evaporation. The outer stem layer has a thick waxy coat (cutin) to prevent any water loss.          J. K. L.

SEE ALSO: LEAVES, STEM

**Caddis fly** (KAHD-ihss) Caddis flies are insects with slender bodies and hairy wing scales which make them look like MOTHS. They have aquatic LARVAE. The larvae spin silken webs and live in cases of sand and pebbles cemented together with strands of web.

SEE: INSECTA

**Caddis fly; larva in case of small stones**

**Cadmium** (CAD-mee-um) Cadmium is a silvery white metal closely related to ZINC in its properties and where it is found. It is never found uncombined in nature. Only one true cadmium mineral is known—*greenockite* (cadmium sulfide). This rare element with poisonous fumes is represented by the chemical symbol, Cd. It is obtained almost exclusively as a by-product of the smelting and refining of zinc ores.

Commercially, cadmium's greatest use is as a coating on iron and steel for protection from corrosion. For this purpose, it is much more practical and efficient than zinc. Cadmium is secondly important as a PIGMENT. Cadmium-yellow (cadmium sulfide) is one of the finest and most permanent pigments. Thirdly, cadmium is a constituent of low-melting-point ALLOYS, used in automatic devices. Recently, cadmium has had atomic energy applications. The cadmium nucleus combines readily with thermal neutrons and was used in the first uranium pile as a reaction moderator. Cadmium's atomic number is 48. Its weight is 112.41.     D. L. D.
SEE ALSO: ELEMENTS

**Caffeine** (KAFF-een) Caffeine is a stimulant found in COFFEE and tea. It is derived from PURINE, a nitrogen compound in vegetable matter.

Two cups of coffee or tea will increase the rate of blood flow, the depth of respiration and the heat production of the body by 10–20%. Caffeine supposedly increases one's mental and physical abilities. There is also some variable effect on the digestive system. Too much caffeine can result in sleeplessness and nervousness.

Since children are very active, they do not need the stimulation of caffeine. In adults' diets, tea and coffee often replace milk, a vital food product.     V. B. I.

**Caisson** (KAY-sun) A caisson is a form that is lowered into the bottom of the water or into the ground. It serves as a shell for a foundation that will be built inside it. Caissons are built of metal, wood or concrete.

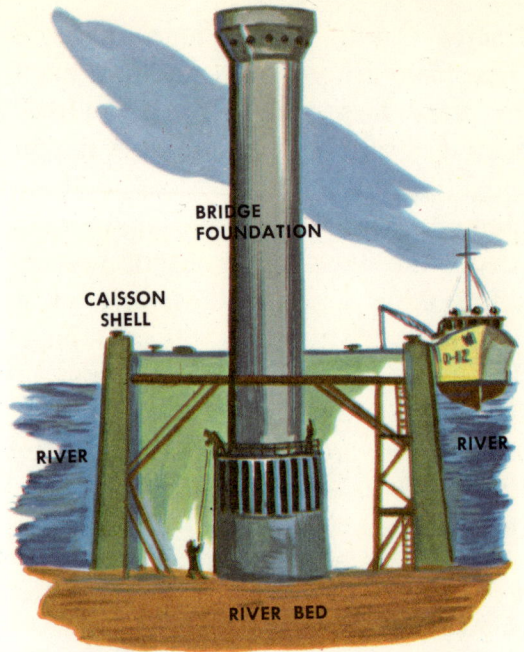

BRIDGE FOUNDATION
CAISSON SHELL
RIVER
RIVER
RIVER BED

**Caissons are used in building supports**

Caissons are used in harbors and rivers to build foundations for lighthouses or to build piers for a bridge. Caissons might be used when a building is to be built on swampy lands.

A *box caisson* is open at the top and rests on a river bed or on rock piles. Tugboats push it into position and then it is sunk.

*Open caissons* are open at both top and bottom and cut into the ocean or river bed as they sink. Dirt and rocks between the walls of the caisson are hoisted out the top.

*Pneumatic caissons* are used in building tunnels under water or for other difficult construction work. The lower section of a pneumatic caisson has cutting edges and a roof. The upper section is open at the top. The foundation is built into the upper section. Its weight helps to drive the lower section into the ground. The water inside the lower section is forced out with compressed air. Then men go into the lower section and dig out the dirt to sink the caisson to the right level.

Before they can begin to work, workmen must sit in an air lock where the pressure is gradually increased until it is the same as the working area. Sudden pressure change could cause death or a painful disorder known as the BENDS.     P. G. B.

**Caisson disease** see Bends

**Calabash** The calabash is a climbing annual vine, native to the tropics. It has gourd-like fruit, as does the unrelated calabash tree which grows nearby.

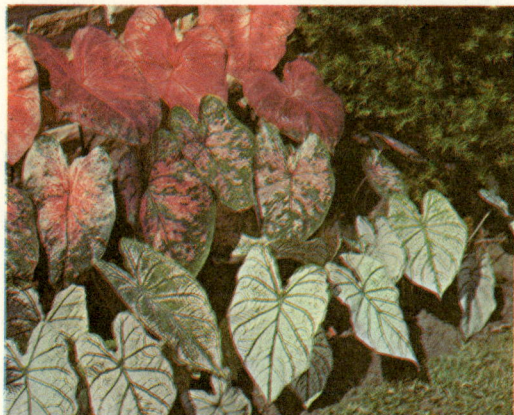

George J. Ball Inc.

Caladiums showing leaves of various colors

**Caladium** (kuh-LAY-dee-um) The caladium is a plant with leaves of many shapes and colors. They may be shaped like hearts or arrowheads, and may be green or mixtures of green, red, or yellow. The caladium is often grown as a house plant.

The caladium originally grew in the rich soil of warm, moist rain forests. The other forest plants shielded it from direct sunshine. When these conditions are matched, the caladium grows best indoors.

The caladium, like its close relative, TARO, rarely blossoms. Instead it spreads by means of a thick underground stem, called a TUBER. Caladium is the genus name commonly used but sometimes the plants are classified as *Colocasia*. The Colocasia originated in the tropics of Asia, while the caladium originated in tropical America. In either case, this PERENNIAL is a hardy, attractive addition to any garden. J. K. L.

**Calamine** Calamine is an important ore of ZINC (zinc silicate) found in Europe and North America. It occurs in CRYSTALS. Calamine also refers to *zinc oxide* used in medicines and cosmetics.

**Calcite** see Rocks

**Calcium** (KAL-see-um) Calcium is a soft metal element which is silver-white in color. It is found in the earth's rocks, in green vegetables and fruits, and in milk. All plants and animals need calcium for their growth.

The diets of both adults and children must have large amounts of calcium compounds to develop strong teeth, sound bones, and healthy blood. Without calcium, the muscles of the body do not work properly, and bones and teeth weaken.

Calcium was discovered in 1808 by SIR HUMPHRY DAVY. Its atomic number is 20, atomic weight 40.08, symbol, Ca. It is rarely found free in nature because it combines actively with water.

Two important calcium compounds are GYPSUM—used to make plaster of Paris—and lime (calcium oxide) from $CaCO_3$.

Pure calcium metal is prepared by melting the oxide or carbonate in an electric furnace.

Interesting chemical changes occur when calcium is mixed with water. The silvery metal oxidizes in minutes to become white calcium hydroxide, and it releases hydrogen gas from the water. L. R. G.

SEE ALSO: ELEMENTS IN THE HUMAN BODY

**Calcium carbonate** (KAL-see-um CAR-bun-ate) Calcium carbonate is one of the most common MINERALS in the earth's crust. It is found in the impure form of marble, limestone, chalk, seashells, coral, egg shells, and is responsible for cave formations.

Pure calcium carbonate, which has a chemical formula of $CaCO_3$, exists in two crystalline forms—*aragonite* and *calcite*. Aragonite is the less stable form, but at lower temperatures and higher pressures it becomes stable. CALCITE is found in the form of pure limestone, white marble, or in transparent crystals, sometimes called *iceland spar*.

Calcium carbonate is used in the manufacture of paint, rubber, dentifrices, paper and chalk. D. L. D.

SEE ALSO: ROCKS, STALACTITE, STALAGMITE

**Calculating machine** see Computer

**Calculus** see Mathematics

OCTOBER  SEPTEMBER

NOVEMBER  AUGUST

365 ¼ DAYS

AVERAGE DISTANCE
92,900,000 MILES

DECEMBER  JULY

91,400,000 MILES  94,400,000 MILES

SUN

JANUARY  JUNE

THE EARTH TRAVELS
ABOUT 30 DEGREES
EVERY MONTH IN ITS
YEARLY PATH AROUND
THE SUN

FEBRUARY  MAY

(18½ MILES/SECOND)
(58 BILLION MILES/YEAR)

MARCH  APRIL

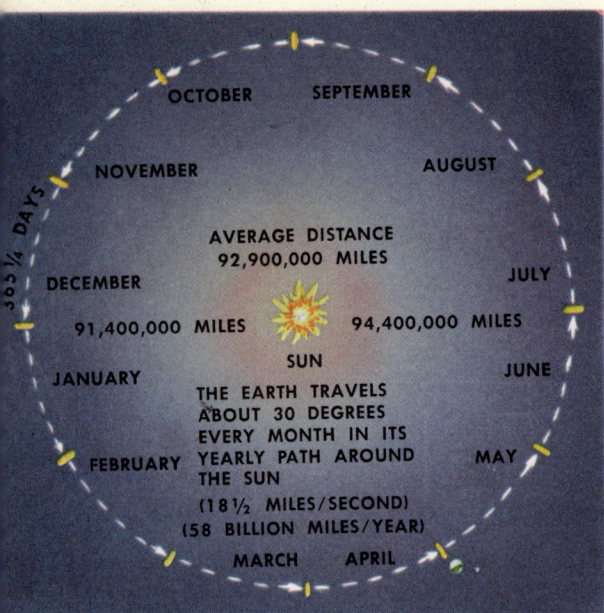

**Calendar** A calendar is a record of the days, weeks, and months of the year. The calendar generally used today has 365 days in each year. So the calendar will be correct, one day is added every fourth year. This year is called *leap year*.

Ancient calendar makers knew that time was divided into days and years. Because days were separated into light and darkness, it was easy to tell how long they were. But it was not simple to figure the length of the year. Eventually, they decided the year must be the amount of time it takes the earth to revolve around the sun. They called this a *solar year*.

The Egyptians were first to measure a year accurately. When a new moon appeared every 29 or 30 days, they called it a *month*. Twelve of these months became a year. This was known as a *lunar calendar*. But it was eleven days short of the time it took the earth to go around the sun. When the Greeks, Babylonians, and Hebrews borrowed this calendar they added an extra month if they found the year too short or seasons coming at the wrong time.

In 46 B.C., the Julian or Old Style calendar appeared. The next major change took place when the Gregorian calendar (named for Pope Gregory XIII) dropped ten days from the year 1582, thus moving all the months ahead. This was called the New Style Calendar.

People are still dissatisfied with the present calendar. A proposed World Calendar has been submitted to the United Nations for approval. It contains a total of 364 days, with an extra day—a holiday—at the year's end. One feature is that any date would always fall on the same day each year. January first and many other holidays would also occur on Sunday.        F. R. W.

**Calendula** (kuh-LENN-juh-luh) Calendula is the name of a group of flowers which have large blossoms made of many yellow or orange petals. These blossoms are sometimes used to flavor soups or stews. The most common calendula is the MARIGOLD, which has been grown in gardens for at least 300 years.

The name *calendula* means "blossoming through the months," which is true of all these plants. They have oblong leaves and somewhat hairy stems. Calendulas grow well in any warm, loose soil. The flowers increase in diameter if the first buds are picked before they open.        J. K. L.

**Californium** (cal-ih-FOR-nee-um) Californium is an element which was very recently discovered by scientists in the radiation laboratory at the University of California. They named this new element in honor of the university and the state. Californium is a member of the actinide series of elements, and possesses chemical properties similar to the elements in that group (ACTINIUM, PROTACTINIUM, etc).

The discovery and production of californium (chemical symbol—Cf) and its ISOTOPES have been based upon artificial nuclear transmutation of lighter elements. Californium, specifically, was discovered by bombarding curium with helium ions, accelerated in a cyclotron. The world's supply of californium is in the range of millionths of a gram. Its application is limited to use in nuclear research.

Californium isotopes present an interesting nuclear property. Especially in $Cf^{252}$ and $Cf^{254}$, decay occurs by spontaneous fission with the discharge of neutrons. $Cf^{252}$ presents possibilities for practical applications as a neutron source. The element number of californium is 98. The atomic weight varies with the isotope.    D. L. D.

SEE ALSO: ACCELERATORS, ELEMENTS

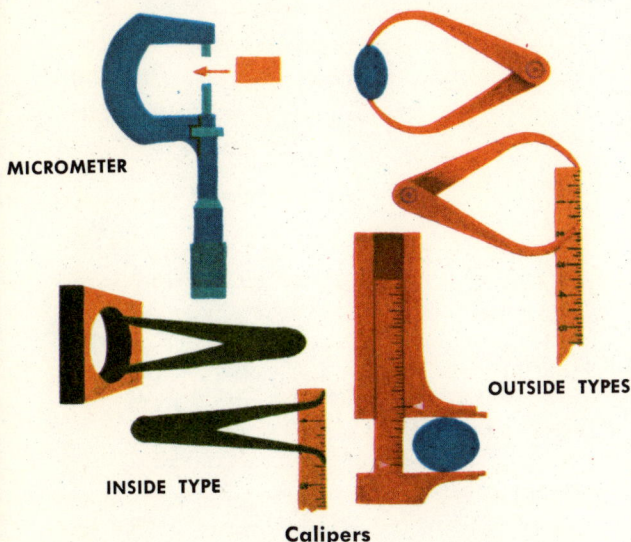

MICROMETER

OUTSIDE TYPES

INSIDE TYPE

Calipers

**Caliper** (KAL-ih-per) A caliper is used to find the size of an object that cannot be measured with a straight line rule. Two arms are set to the size of an object and then compared to a ruler.

A caliper can measure outside diameters and thicknesses of tree trunks, balls, rods, bars, etc. The size of an opening in an object is measured with a caliper whose arms touch inside surfaces.

Some calipers have a scale which shows the measurement directly when the caliper arms touch an object's surface. Measurements of fine machine parts are taken with a screw micrometer caliper.    F. R. W.

SEE ALSO: MEASUREMENT

**Calm, regions of** Regions of calm are places in the ATMOSPHERE where there is no horizontal air motion or wind. They are the opposite of the JET STREAMS.

**Calorie** The calorie is a unit for measuring HEAT energy. It is used to describe the necessary heat needed to raise the temperature of water a desired amount. In food chemistry, it refers to the heat energy which a particular food can yield.

More precisely, one calorie of heat applied to one gram of water raises its temperature one degree Centigrade. Water requires more heat to raise its temperature one degree than does the same amount of other common substances. For example, one gram of copper takes only one-eleventh calorie to rise one degree Centigrade. One gram of aluminum takes about one-fifth calorie. The large Calorie (with a capital "C") is 1000 small calories.

The gram-calorie is a very small unit of heat energy. One gram is only one-four hundred fifty-fourth ($\frac{1}{454}$) of a pound. Because the calorie is so small, food chemists use the large Calorie to measure the energy in foods.

One large Calorie (or kilogram-calorie) of heat applied to 1,000 grams (about 2.2 pounds) of water raises its temperature one degree Centigrade. A slice of bread containing 100 Calories actually equals 100,000 small calories.    J. H. D.

SEE ALSO: BRITISH THERMAL UNIT, CALORIMETRY

**Calorimetry** (kal-uh-RIMM-uh-tree) Calorimetry refers to the measurement of the quantity of heat exchanged by a test body with the apparatus called the calorimeter. The measurement of heat ENERGY is carried out in a *calorimeter*. One kind of calorimeter has two metal cans, one small can is placed inside a larger can. The small can is held in place with a large fiber washer. An air space exists between the containers. A wooden lid is provided with a hole for inserting a stirring rod and another for a thermometer. The air space between the walls helps reduce the loss or gain of heat from the surroundings.

If a definite weight of cool water is placed inside the colorimeter and its temperature measured, and some heated material added, it is possible to find out how much heat is received by the cold water. The number of calories of heat received by the water and the container holding it may be calculated.

The functioning of a calorimeter is based on the Law of Conservation of Energy. The heat lost by a warm body equals the heat gained by the cooler body which receives it.

One CALORIE of heat applied to one gram of water raises its temperature one degree C. Only a fraction of a calorie is required to raise the temperature of one gram of most common materials one degree C. This quantity of heat is called the *specific heat* of a substance. To find the total calories of heat energy needed to raise the temperature of any mass any number of degrees, multiply the mass, in grams, by the specific heat by the change in temperature, in degrees C.

The calorimeter provides a way to measure the specific heat of various materials. It may be used also to find the heat required to melt a gram of ice.

Special types of calorimeters are used to measure the heat values of fuels or foods. Often a *bomb calorimeter* is used. The fuel (or food) with a supply of oxygen is burned in an enclosed metal container surrounded by water. The heat given off is received by the water. From the rise in temperature of the water, the heat value of the fuel in calories may be calculated. Foods are handled in the same way, but they are expressed in kilogram-calories, which are 1,000 times larger than gram-calories.                J. H. D.

SEE ALSO: HEAT OF FUSION, HEAT OF VAPORIZATION

**Calyx** (KAY-lix) The calyx is the part of a FLOWER which protects the BUD. It is usually green and thicker than the petals of the flower. After the flower opens, the calyx may fall off. More often, however, it forms a little cup around the petals. Sometimes the calyx remains after the petals of the flower have dropped off.

The calyx may have separate parts, called *sepals,* or it may be one continuous piece. The SEPALS are rarely stalked. When the sepals match the petals, an inexperienced observer often thinks that the flower has no calyx. Actually only a few kinds of flowering plants lack them.            J. K. L.

SEE ALSO: ANGIOSPERMS, PETAL

**Cambium** (KAM-bee-um) Cambium is that part of the plant which helps it to grow in width. Plants have only four areas of cells with the power to divide and increase the size of the plant. The stem tip and root tip help the plant to grow taller and the roots to extend deeper into the soil.

The growth of a plant in width, or circumference, is accomplished by two kinds of tissue with the ability to multiply—the cork cambium and the vascular cambium.

The vascular cambium separates the PHLOEM from the XYLEM cells. When bark is peeled from a trunk of a tree the cambial layer is exposed. This cambium makes new xylem and phloem cells throughout the growing season.

Cork cambium is found between the cork and phloem in the bark of trees. It produces cork cells which protect the plant from internal loss of water and external attack by insects and other enemies. Without cambial tissue all plants would live one year and die. All secondary growth of BIENNIALS and PERENNIALS is produced by the cambium.            H. J. C.

SEE ALSO: ANNUAL RINGS

**Camel** The camel is a tall animal with a humped back, long legs, a goose-like neck and small head. It is used for riding and for carrying heavy loads across the desert. It is often called "The Ship of the Desert."

There are two different kinds of camels, the Arabian and the Bactrian. The Arabian camel (*dromedary*), found in Arabia, India and North Africa, has one hump on its back and is used mainly for riding. It can run as fast as ten miles an hour over the soft sands of the desert, and has been known to carry a rider one hundred miles in one day. The Bactrian camel, found in Asia, has two humps on its back and is used mainly for

Courtesy Society For Visual Education, Inc.
**Arabian camel**

**Bactrian camel**

carrying heavy loads. It is stronger and shorter than the Arabian camel, and has thick long hair on its humps, neck, shoulders and the top of its head. Bactrian camels can carry as much as one thousand pounds, traveling at a rate of two or three miles per hour. Of the four million camels in the world, three million are Arabian and one million are Bactrian.

The camel's body is well-suited to life on the desert. The soles of its broad two-toed feet are covered with thick callous pads which keep it from sinking into the sand. Its eyes, protected by long lashes and over-hanging lids, are set high on its head, enabling it to see long distances. The slit nostrils of its nose may be closed against blowing sand and dust. The stiff skin of its upper lip may be used to break off spiny desert plants which the camel then chews with its powerful teeth. Thick callous pads at the joints of its legs and on its chest protect the camel from the hot sand when it is resting.

The camel's humps have no bony structure. They consist of extra food stored in the form of fat. When the camel is well-fed, its humps are large and full. When it is not well-fed, its body uses the food stored in the humps and they become flabby and small.

The camel is able to go without water for many days. It can drink great quantities of water at one time. Because it does not sweat, it does not lose this water very rapidly. Water is also produced in the camel's body as the fat in its humps is changed to energy.

The mother camel has one baby born in the spring. The baby, called a *calf* or *colt,* has a small body but has legs almost as long and thick as those of its mother. It is full-grown when it is seventeen years old, and may live as long as thirty or forty years.

The camel is one of the oldest known living mammals. It has served man for over five thousand years. Camels have been with man for so long, there are no records of how or when they were first tamed.

People could not live on the deserts of Africa, Arabia and Asia without the camel. They not only depend on it for transportation, but they also drink its milk, eat its flesh, and use its woolly hair to make cloth. Camels do not become fond of their masters and usually have mean dispositions. D. J. A.

**Camellia** (kuh-MEEL-yuh) The camellia is an evergreen tree or bush. Its lovely flowers are often worn as corsages. The pink, red, or white flowers are waxy and the leaves are a shiny, dark green.

The camelia is native to Asia and belongs to the tea (*Thaceae*) family. In the North, camellias are grown in cool greenhouses, but in the South they grow outdoors in moist shady spots, where they blossom in the winter and spring. PROPAGATION is by cuttings.

The dried leaves of *Camellia sasanqua* have a pleasant taste and are often mixed with tea leaves. The oil from *Camellia drupifera* is used in medicine. *Camellia japonica* and *Camellia creticulata* are odorless and are the kinds most commonly grown for their blossoms. J. M. C.

**Camellia**

**MAKING A CAMERA THAT WORKS**

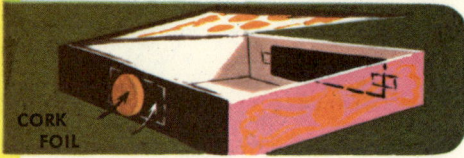

CORK
FOIL

**Material: Cigar box, cork, foil, photographic film, developer**

1   A homemade camera may be constructed which will take pictures on film. This project is for the more experienced photographer.

2   Drill a half-inch hole in one end of a cigar box. Find a cork that fits tightly into this hole. On the inside of the box tape a one inch by one inch piece of foil over the hole. Take a needle and punch a clean hole directly in the center of the foil.

3   In a dark room tape a piece of photographic film on the end of the box directly opposite the needle hole. Fasten the lid of the box tightly with tape, and be certain the cork is in before going out in the daylight.

4   Point the camera at an object. Rest it on something to keep it from jiggling and distorting the picture. Remove the cork for one or two seconds depending on the brightness of the day. Quickly replace the cork, return to a dark room, and develop the film.

**Camera** A camera is a light-tight enclosure used to permanently record images on a light-sensitive EMULSION. The emulsion is generally coated on FILM or a glass plate. The camera, a basic photographic tool, consists of six principal parts:

1) *Body*—a metal, wood, or plastic box which contains the other parts;

2) *Viewfinder*—a wire frame or optical device for framing the area of the subject being photographed;

3) *Holder*—film or plate-holding device at the back of the body, which, when activated, releases the exposed film or plate;

4) *Lens*—an optical element at the front of the body which focuses the image upon the emulsion;

5) *Aperture*—either a fixed or variable opening attached to the lens which controls the amount of light entering the camera body;

6) *Shutter*—a mechanism which allows light to pass through the aperture for a given length of time.

A *still camera* requires film which, when exposed, is either printed on paper as individual photographs, or directly mounted as projection slides. A *motion picture camera* contains a mechanism which advances the film continuously past the lens. The printed film is projected on a screen to produce an illusion of motion of the subject.

**HOW DOES A CAMERA WORK?**

**Material: cracker box, tissue paper, candle**

1   Cover an open end of a cracker box with white tissue paper. Tape it securely in place to avoid wrinkles in the paper. Make a pin hole in the center of the closed end of the box.

2   Take the "camera" into a dark room. Set a lighted candle two feet in front of the pinhole. Stand behind the "camera" and observe the pattern on the tissue paper.

3   Since light travels in straight lines the top of the flame will show on the bottom of the picture on the tissue paper. The image is upside down.

The more common types of still cameras are:

*Box*—simplest of all—a light-tight box with fixed focus, aperture, and shutter speed;

*Folding*—similar to the box, but a collapsible bellows replaces the front part of the box to make the camera more compact. Lens focus, aperture, and shutter speed may be varied;

*Miniature*—a small, compact camera having many fine features. Film is so small that pictures must be enlarged when printed;

*Reflex*—a box-type camera with a viewfinder that reflects the film size image;

*Press*—a large, bulky, folding-type camera used primarily for newspaper and magazine photography;

*View*—larger than the press camera. This camera is mounted on a stand and usually is found in a commercial photography studio.　　　　　E. I. D.

SEE ALSO: LENS, MAN-MADE; MOTION PICTURES; PHOTOGRAPHY

**Camomile** Camomile is a PERENNIAL plant of the THISTLE family. The dried flowers are used in home remedies.

**Camouflage**　　(KAMM-uh-flahzh) Camouflage means to hide an object or to confuse an enemy as to the object's presence, location, or characteristics. Camouflage, which takes advantage of natural means of concealment, or provides artificial ones, is based on PROTECTIVE COLORATION—a principle found in the animal world. The zebra's pattern makes it less visible in its natural surroundings, as does the white color of the polar bear against an ice background. The CHAMELEON's ability to change color is another example.

Man used camouflage for security in his tree-top and cliff dwellings. The Greeks used this deception in capturing the city of Troy. Troops for battle were concealed within the famous wooden Trojan horse.

In World War I, camouflage was formally adopted by the combat forces, and by World War II, it had reached even greater importance because of air reconnaissance.

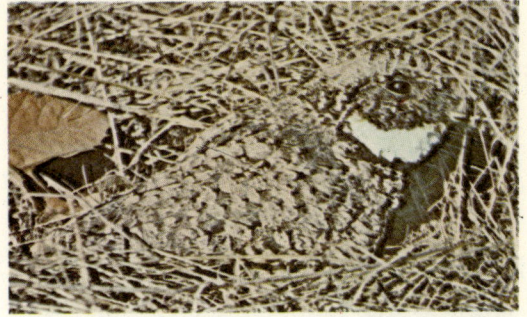
Courtesy Society For Visual Education, Inc.
The soldier and the whippoorwill use camouflage to blend with their surroundings

Concealment and confusion of targets was of vital necessity on land, at sea, and in the air. During World War II, landing operations were constantly carried out under smoke screens which hindered observation and foiled air attacks. The planting of trees and simulating foliage by covering net screens with actual or artificial foliage are common camouflage techniques. Painting is another device—either solid painting to blend an object in with its background, or disruptive painting to confuse the shape of an obvious or very large object. If a "dummy" tank to be used as a decoy is "carelessly" disguised, and is then identified by the enemy as an actual tank, then camouflage scores by illusion. The night blackout and dispersion of troops are still considered useful methods of camouflage.

The science of camouflage is a very progressive one, for it must keep pace with the latest scientific developments (such as missiles, rockets, infra-red and filter photography) in order to be effective.　D. L. D.

**Camphor** (KAMM-fer) Camphor is a whitish compound from the camphor tree—native to China, Japan and Formosa. Camphor is obtained by DISTILLATION of the finely-ground wood and leaves. It is then refined down to commercial gum camphor. It has a penetrating, characteristic odor and a pungent, aromatic taste.

Camphor is used medicinally as a liniment, analgesic, and as a gastrointestinal drug. It is important in the manufacture of celluloid and nitrocellulose compounds, in perfumes, photographic film, insect repellent, and as a retardant for tarnish on silver and mildew on wood. D. L. D.

**Canal** A canal is a man-made waterway used for shipping or for irrigating land. Ship canals are built for three main reasons. A canal may connect two big bodies of water. A canal may be built around a section of a river with falls or rapids. A canal may provide a waterway to a city which has no outlet to a river or a sea.

The Egyptians built a canal in 2000 B.C., joining the Nile River and the Red Sea. One of the longest and oldest canals was begun around 500 B.C. in China. The Erie Canal (1825) was the first significant canal in the United States. It connected Lake Erie and the Hudson River and was important in the westward development of the country.

Usually, canals are built wide enough to allow two ships to pass each other, and are deep enough to retain a 1½ foot margin of water beneath the largest of ships.

**A simple lock-type canal**

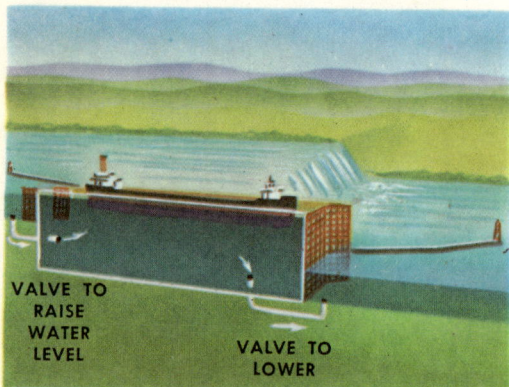

VALVE TO RAISE WATER LEVEL

VALVE TO LOWER

A *lock,* first used by the Dutch in the 14th century, is a water elevator. A watertight gate is located at each end of the lock. The gates close after a boat enters the lock. The ship is then moved up or down by adjusting the water level. Important canals are the Panama Canal, the Suez Canal, and the canals in the St. Lawrence Seaway. P. F. D.

**Male (left) and female canaries**

**Canary** The canary is one of the most popular and cheerful of all birds. Its beautiful song has led to its place in the home to bring cheer and melody. The canary is a member of the FINCH family. It is named for the Canary Islands, where it lived wild.

The tame canary, which is bred for excellence of song, is superior to the wild canaries in singing ability. Both wild and domestic canaries are bright yellow, orange, reddish, or pale yellow.

Canaries eat mostly seeds, but they also need fresh green food. Their cages should be clean and large enough for flying exercise. They need water for drinking and for bathing. V. V. N.

**Canaveral, Cape** see Cape Canaveral

**Cancer (constellation)** Cancer is a group of stars which has been imagined to look like a crab. This CONSTELLATION can be seen in the spring. Cancer is one of the signs of the ZODIAC.

The sun reaches the sign of Cancer about June 21st. At this time the sun can be seen directly overhead at noon at an imaginary line called the *Tropic of Cancer.* This line marks the most northern limit of the places on Earth where the sun can be seen directly overhead at noon.

On a very clear evening the constellation Cancer looks like a silvery cloud between two faint stars. When a telescope is used to look at the cloud it can be seen to be a

Cancer, the Crab

cluster of faint stars. It is sometimes called *Praesepe,* or the *Manger.* The two stars beside it are called *Aselli,* the donkeys who are eating out of the Manger. Sometimes the cluster is called the *Beehive.* The star cluster of Cancer has long been a weather signal. When it can be seen, fair weather is ahead. It is held that before a storm, the Manger cannot be seen at all.

The Greeks believed that this star pattern was a memorial to the crab which Juno had sent to bite Hercules when he was fighting with the monster Hydra.          C. L. K.

**Cancer (disease)** Cancer is a growth of cells which often form malignant tumors. Unless something is done to stop the cell growth, cancer may take a person's life. The *malignant* tumor is in contrast to the *benign* type. A benign tumor grows more slowly than the malignant variety and does not interfere with a person's well-being or take his life.

The basic cellular structure of a cancer is the *epithelial* cell, one of the many kinds of cells which make up the body. It is an epithelial cell gone wrong—one that does not live by the rules which govern all other cells. The epithelial cells are the kind which make up the skin. They line all canals of the body to which air has access and organs having a very special kind of work to do, such as the liver and kidneys.

Cancer has a great tendency to have its cells travel to distant parts of the body and start a new tumor wherever they land. Among the particular characteristics of malignant cancer cells are: 1) Their cen-

ters or nuclei are much larger than the average nucleus. 2) When cancer cells break down they form LACTIC ACID, whereas ordinary cells under similar circumstances form carbon dioxide and water. 3) They do not require as much oxygen to live. 4) Cancer cells have no control over dividing or multiplying themselves. 5) Singly or in groups, they can invade neighboring structures; when they do so, they outlive the cells in the tissue they have invaded. 6) When cancer cells are cut out of the body, the whole process of growth can start all over. This happens because maybe just one cell, visible only with a microscope, was left behind. When this happens the tumor is called *carcinoma.* Cancers can start any place in the body. In the bony structure or lymph glands they are given a different name—*sarcoma.*

Cancer grows at different rates of speed in different parts of the body. In the skin, it grows slowly and rarely spreads to other parts of the body. Cancer may occur at any age. It is more frequent in older adults, but it is more rapid in growth and very often fatal in younger persons.

Many theories have been advanced as to the cause of cancer, partly because there are many different kinds of cancer. A single cause for all forms of cancer has not yet been determined. Mechanical injury or constant irritation is a contributing cause in some cancers. Heredity has been shown experimentally to be important in influencing the onset of cancer and the age at which one develops it. One of the latest and perhaps the most promising idea is that various viruses play an important part in the cause.

One fact about cancer, which has been proven repeatedly, is that early and prompt attack on the invading disease offers the best chance for prolonging the life of the affected individual.          H. K. S.

SEE ALSO: EPITHELIAL TISSUE, TUMOR

**Photo-micrograph of carcinoma in tonsil tissue. The dark spots are the nuclei of cells**
Photo Courtesy Chas. Pfizer & Co., Inc.

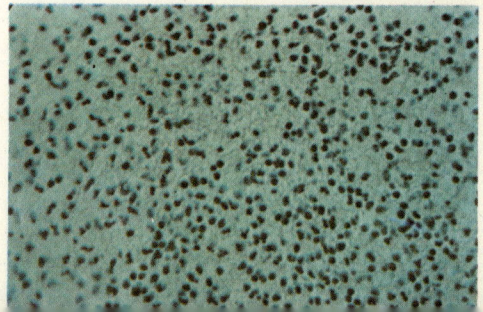

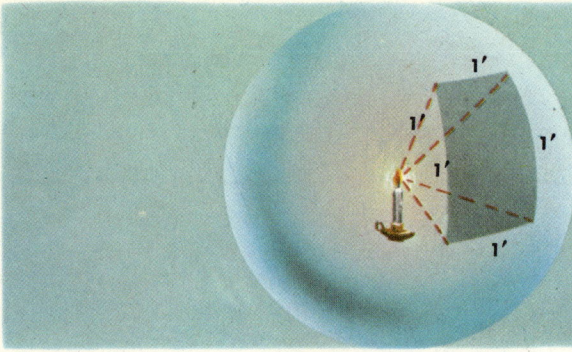

The sphere represents a transparent ball which has a radius of one foot. A light source of one candle is placed at the exact center. When a one-foot square is drawn on the surface of the sphere, and lines are drawn from the corners of this to the light source, a solid angle, or *steradian*, is formed. The intensity of light emitted through this angle is one *lumen*, and the amount of light falling on the surface of the sphere is one *foot-candle*

**Candle power** Long ago, a candle which was made and burned under certain conditions was used as a standard for measuring light intensity. Candle power is the light-producing power, called *luminous intensity,* of a standard candle. A light source of one candle emits one candle power of LIGHT energy. An instrument called the PHOTOMETER is used to measure candle power.

In 1940, the United States Bureau of Standards adopted a more specific candle reference. A special box containing platinum is heated to its melting point of 1773° C. The light produced by this standard is defined as 60 candles.

A light source of one candle will emit 12.56 lumens. A *lumen* is defined as a unit of luminous flux or the amount of light coming from a fixed light source of one candle through a solid angle of one *steradian*. There are 12.56 steradians to a point source. The relationship of all these terms is best understood with the aid of the illustration above.

The *foot-candle* is the measure of illumination and can be defined as one lumen equally distributed over one square foot. Illumination (I) is calculated by dividing the candle power (C) by the distance squared ($D^2$) from the light source. The equation of this relationship is:

$$I = \frac{C}{D^2}$$

The luminous efficiency of a light source is computed by dividing the candle power by the electrical power (watts) consumed in operating the light. A 100-watt incandescent lamp produces 114 candle power, while a fluorescent lamp of the same power input will produce 320 candle power. Almost three 100-watt incandescent lamps would be required to produce the same quantity of candle power as would be produced by the 100-watt fluorescent lamp.    E. I. D.

**Evergreen candytuft**

**Candytuft** The candytuft has a wide flat blossom made up of many small, four-petalled flowers. These plants first came from the countries along the Mediterranean Sea. The flowers are white, red or purple, and some have a very pleasant smell. The common candytuft, about ten inches tall, is often grown as a garden border.

All candytufts have the shorter stemmed flowers in the center of the blossom. The two outer petals of the flower are longer than the inner. The sap has a strong odor, and the whole plant feels soft and downy. Some candytufts are shrubs, others are evergreens or PERENNIALS, but the common varieties are ANNUALS.    J. K. L.

**Cane** see Grasses, Palm

**Cane sugar** see Sugar

**Canis Major and Canis Minor** (KAY-niss) Canis Major and Canis Minor are two groups of stars that have been imagined to represent dogs. Canis Major means the *Greater Dog*. Canis Minor means the *Lesser Dog*. They are not very large CONSTELLA-TIONS, but each of them has one very bright star. Canis Major contains the brightest star in the sky, SIRIUS. These two constellations can be seen in the wintertime, near the famous hunter constellation ORION.

The stars of Canis Major are usually pictured as a dog standing on its hind legs. Sirius is either the dog's nose or his jaw. Canis Minor has fewer stars. Its bright star, PROCYON, is the dog's body and three smaller stars form the curve of its head. Sirius, Procyon, and BETELGEUSE, the bright star in Orion, form an equilateral triangle sometimes called the *Winter Triangle*.

The most famous explanation of these star dogs is that they belong to the hunter, ORION. Other stories say that Canis Major is a memorial to a very fast dog, Laelops, who ran a race with a fox. Another story is that they are the goddess Diana's hunting dogs.

The people of Egypt, Assyria, Phoenicia, Chaldea, Greece, and Rome all recognized these star patterns as dogs. The Egyptians worshipped Sirius, which they called the "dog star." When Sirius made its first appearance on the horizon before dawn, they knew that the time had come for the Nile to flood—a very important event to Egyptian farmers. Procyon means "before the dog." Ancient people predicted changes in weather when they observed Procyon rising into the sky, because Procyon appeared just before Sirius.

In ancient times Sirius was in the sky during the day in the summertime. It was invisible, but the people believed that Sirius combined its heat with the sun's heat to make midsummer almost unbearable. They called this period "dog days." C. L. K.

**Canker worm** Canker worms are also called *measuring* WORMS. They are MOTH larvae and very destructive to leaves.

**Canna** see Plants, tropical

**Cannibal fish** see Tropical fish

**Canning** see Food preservation

**Cannon** see Weapons

**Cantaloupe** see Melons

**Canterbury bell** (KAN-ter-bury bell) Canterbury bells have flowers shaped like bells which bloom along the sides of its tall stalk. The blossoms are white, pink, or blue. The hairy leaves of this plant are six to nine inches long.

The Canterbury bell is an HERB from southern Europe. It is a BIENNIAL that is grown from seed. The seeds are sown in summer. In the fall, the young plants are transplanted to a semi-shady place in the garden. They prefer medium-rich soil. A mulch of dried leaves provides winter protection. The following June or July the plants bloom. M. R. L.

**Cantilever** see Bridges

Canis Major, the Big Dog, and Canis Minor, the Little Dog, have major stars included in their figures

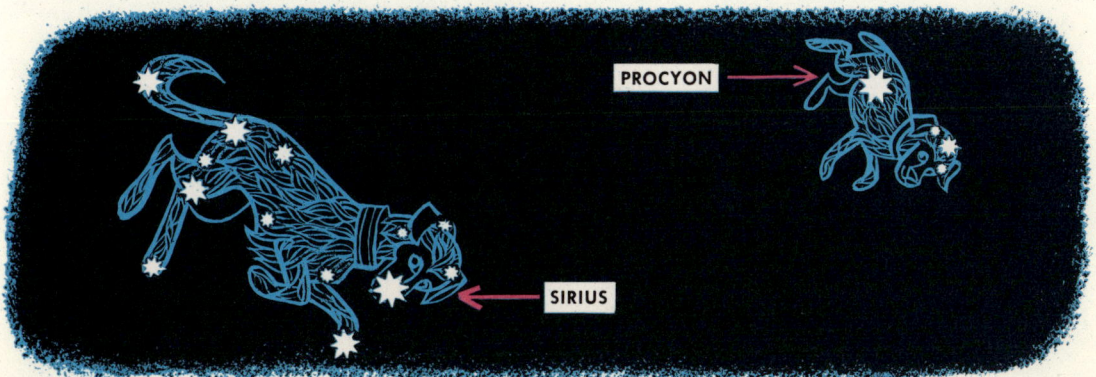

**Canyon** Canyons are large openings in the ground that are deep and have high, steep sides. They are found on the bottom of the oceans as well as on the land. Canyons found on the OCEAN floor may be many times larger than those that have been formed on the continents.

Ocean canyons may be as much as 24,000 feet below the ocean floor. The greatest canyon on the earth is more than a mile deep in places but never goes below sea level because it is cut through a plateau that is 6,000 to 8,000 feet above sea level.

When canyons are formed by the cutting action of a river or glacier, the various layers in the top or crust may be exposed. These layers may give clues about the geological history of the earth.

The Grand Canyon of Arizona, perhaps the best known of all canyons, tells the history of that section of the United States through the many rocks and layers of land that have been exposed on the sides of the canyon by the downward EROSION of the Colorado River.                     J. D. B.
SEE ALSO: GEOLOGY

**Capacitor** see Condenser

**Cape** A piece of land that extends or juts out into an ocean or a lake is called a *cape*. Some of the more well-known capes are Cape of Good Hope, Cape Cod, and Cape Horn.

**Cape Canaveral** Cape Canaveral is a fifteen thousand acre piece of land, mostly sandspit, on the eastern coast of Florida. It has been the site of the Air Force Missile Test Center since 1950. MISSILES of war for all the military services are tested there and peacetime research SATELLITES and space probes are launched there. The test range extends from the Cape, some six thousand miles south into the Atlantic Ocean.
SEE ALSO: ASTRONAUTICS

**Capella** see Auriga

**Caper** (KAY-puhr) Capers are the flower buds of a Mediterranean white flowering shrub. The bud is picked and pickled for use in salads and meat sauces.

**Capillarity** (kapp-uh-LAIR-uh-tee) When the surface of a liquid is "free," as in a large bowl of water or bath tub, it is considered to be flat or horizontal except where the water comes into contact with the sides of the container. Here, the surface of the liquid is curved. It may be curved up or down, a small or large amount, depending on the kind of liquid. The curvature of the liquid is a direct result of what is called *surface tension,* and this results in actions called *capillary phenomena.*

Water, in contact with a vertical surface of glass, is curved upward because of the ADHESION of water molecules to the glass. Mercury, under the same conditions, is curved downward because of strong cohesive forces in mercury. The angle that the liquid makes with the solid surface is called the *angle of capillarity.*

When a glass tube with a very small hole (called a *capillary tube*), open at both ends, is placed vertically in a container filled with water, the water in the tube tends to rise above the level of the liquid in the container. However, if a glass tube of the same bore is placed in a container of mercury, the mercury in the tube will be at a level which is lower than that of the mercury in the container. This is because the surface of the water curves upward where it contacts the glass, thus tending to pull more water up into the tube. Since the surface of the mercury curves downward where it contacts the glass, it tends to push the mercury out of the tube.

The heated water does not rise as high as the cold water because the surface tension of the heated water is less than that of the cold water. Thus, it can be seen that the amount of CAPILLARY rise depends on the diameter of the tube and on the surface tension of the liquid.          A. E. L.
SEE ALSO: SURFACE TENSION

## ✳ THINGS TO DO

### EXPERIMENTING WITH ADHESION AND COHESION TO SHOW CAPILLARITY

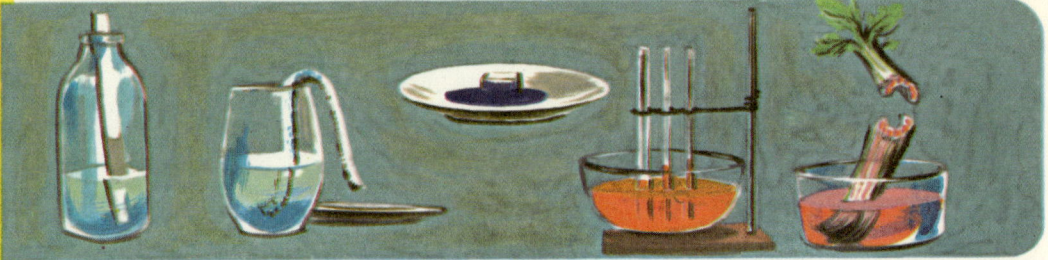

1   Put an inch of water in a milk bottle. Place one end of a strip of blotting paper in the water with the other end hanging out of the mouth of the bottle. Notice the movement of water up the blotter.

2   Set a cube of sugar in a saucer containing a film of ink solution. Can you see the ink go up the sugar?

3   Place one end of a lamp wick in a glass of water. Let the other end hang out. Put a pan under this end to catch the water as it comes up the wick and drips off the exposed end.

4   Set the ends of several glass tubes with varying widths in a colored solution. Observe the water rise.

5   Place a stalk of fresh celery in a glass of red dye. After one hour cut a cross-section of the celery and notice the red circles.

6   Explanation: Water molecules adhere to the molecules of the material above it—the blotter, glass tube, sugar, lamp wick, and celery. This pull is greater than the cohesion or sticking together of one water molecule to the adjoining water molecule.

**Capillary** (KAP-puh-lair-ee) Capillaries are the smallest of all blood vessels which transport the BLOOD throughout the body. Blood vessels are divided into four main groups—arteries, arterioles, capillaries and veins. These groups are parts of one complete system. The *arteries* are the largest and strongest vessels in the CIRCULATORY SYSTEM. They branch off into smaller vessels called *arterioles*. From the arterioles arise many tiny hair-like tubes called *capillaries*. These tubes are microscopic in size. They intertwine with each other to form a network of vessels.

Capillaries enter into nearly every tissue of the body. The walls of these vessels are so thin that fluids can pass through them into the cells. It is through these vessels that the actual exchange between the tissues and the blood takes place. The blood brings life-sustaining foods to the cells, collects waste materials from them, then continues through the veins and back to the heart. The capillary network functions as an exchange center and as a connection between the arterial and the venous system.

The smallest capillaries are those in the brain and in the mucous membranes of the intestines. The largest are those in the skin and the marrow of the bones.

The blood supply in the various organs of the body depends upon the number of capillaries and the size of the meshes which are found among them.

Organs which function continually tend to have a larger capillary network than those which are less active.   G. A. D.

SEE ALSO: ARTERY, VEIN

TODAY'S HEALTH, published by AMERICAN MEDICAL ASSOCIATION

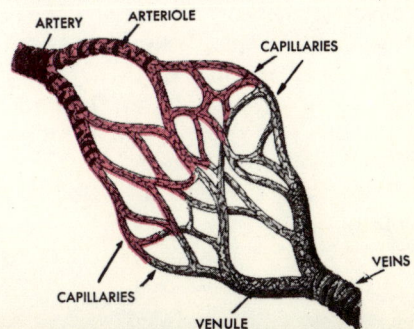

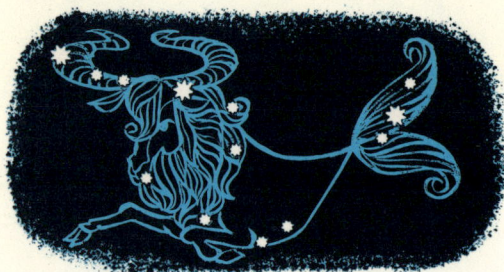
**Capricornus, the Goat**

**Capricornus** (kapp-ruh-KOR-nus) Capricornus is the CONSTELLATION that is sometimes called the *Goat,* or the *Sea Goat.* This group of stars looks like a bent triangle. It is a rather faint, autumn constellation and is one of the signs of the ZODIAC.

When the sun is in the sign of Capricorn, in December, it is highest overhead in the southern part of the world. The imaginary line that marks the southern boundary of the path of the sun is called the "Tropic of Capricorn."

According to one legend, the goat represents the god Bacchus, who assumed the shape of a goat one day to escape a giant named Typhon. Some ancient star maps picture Capricornus as a Sea Goat, or a creature with the head of a goat and the tail of a fish. This figure was supposed to represent the god Pan, who assumed this shape one day as he was frolicking in the Nile. Some stories mix the two legends and say that the sea goat was the shape that Pan took to escape from Typhon.     C. L. K.

**Capsicum** see Cayenne

**Capsule** (CAP-suhl) A capsule is a seed-pod that is divided into sections or compartments. When the SEEDS are ripe, the dry capsule opens so that the seeds may be shaken out.

Capsules are not all alike. The carrot capsule, for example, has only two sections with one seed in each section. The poppy capsule has many sections, each with a small hole at the top covered by a valve, and each containing many seeds.

A capsule is the fruit of a flower with a compound ovary.     J. M. C.
SEE ALSO: ANGIOSPERMS, FRUIT, PLANT

**Capybara** The capybara is a large South American rodent. It looks like a GUINEA PIG but may weigh as much as 100 lbs. It lives along river banks and lake shores.
SEE: RODENTIA

**Carat** Carat is a unit of measure that is used by jewelers when they weigh precious stones and metals such as diamonds. It is also used to show the amount of pure gold in a mixture made of gold and other materials.

The word *carat* originally came from an Arabic word that referred to a bean or seed of a certain coral tree. These beans were used in the East to weigh gold. As a unit of weight for precious stones, the carat has been standardized by the United States government at 200 milligrams or $\frac{1}{5}$ of a gram. A two carat diamond thus weighs 400 milligrams or $\frac{2}{5}$ of one gram. This weight, 200 milligrams, has been accepted by most leading governments of the world.

Carat used to mean a 24th part in the weight of the gold marc. It now means just a 24th part and is used to express the weight of gold in an ALLOY. 18 carats means 18 parts of 24 are pure gold—$18_{24}$ or $\frac{3}{4}$ of the material is gold. 12 carat gold is $12_{24}$ or $\frac{1}{2}$ pure gold.     J. D. B.
SEE ALSO: GEM

**Caraway** Caraway is an HERB. It has been known for centuries for its tiny, pungent seed. Caraway seed is used for seasoning foods such as soups, cheese, meats, salads and vegetables. Its most common use is in rye bread.

Caraway grows in Europe and Asia and in northern and northwestern United States. It is a hardy BIENNIAL that sows itself year after year. It is found growing in any kind of soil. Caraway will grow two feet tall, has beautiful, feathery leaves, and creamy or yellowish-white flowers.     J. K. K.

**Caraway**

**Carbohydrates** (car-boh-HY-drates) Carbohydrates is a term applied to SUGARS, starches, cellulose, and many related compounds. Carbohydrates are used for food by plants and animals.

Plants are the only living things that manufacture carbohydrates. They take the carbon dioxide from the air and the water from the soil, and, through the process of PHOTOSYNTHESIS, they build these two products into the cellulose of wood, cotton, and grasses, or into the sugar and starch of potatoes, rice, and other roots and grains.

Until recently the term carbohydrate included only those compounds which contained carbon and the ratio of two hydrogen atoms to one oxygen atom. For example, dextrose, a simple sugar, is symbolized $C_6H_{12}O_6$. However, new substances were discovered whose properties and characteristics classified them as carbohydrates, but they deviated from the required hydrogen to oxygen ratio. Therefore, the new definition of carbohydrate is a matter of convenience rather than of exact definition.

Although the properties of many carbohydrates differ enormously from one substance to another, they do have a common basis, and STARCHES and CELLULOSE can be broken down by different methods into the same crystalline sugar.    D. L. D.

**Carbolic acid** (kahr-BAHL-ick) Carbolic acid is a colorless, crystalline solid which has an easily recognized odor. Its scientific name is *phenol*. Phenol is extremely poisonous. It destroys human skin and is a nerve poison.

Phenol is prepared by the distillation of COAL TAR, or, on a large commercial scale, by a synthetic process. It is used chiefly as a disinfectant, and in the preparation of some plastics. *Picric acid,* a derivative of phenol, is an ingredient in many high explosives. Phenol also has application in the manufacture of dyes, medicines, plant hormones, weed killers, and tanning agents.    D. L. D.

**Carbon** Carbon is a common chemical element. Large amounts of it are found in the free state in nature. The DIAMOND is the purest form of carbon. It exists as an eight-sided CRYSTAL. When pure, it is colorless, transparent, and brilliant. Inferior quality diamonds are used industrially for glass cutting, grinding, and on the points of drills. This is because the diamond is the hardest substance known. Diamonds can only be cut by other diamonds, and polished with diamond powder.

A piece of strawberry shortcake contains the three main types of carbohydrates—*disaccharides,* or double sugars (in the form of *lactose* from the whipped cream); *fructose,* a simple sugar from the strawberries; and starch, a *polysaccharide,* in the cake.

When this is eaten, the salivary enzymes change the cooked starch to a double sugar, as the first step in the breakdown. In the alimentary canal, the double sugars are hydrolyzed, or turned into simple sugars, by the action of enzymes. These simple sugars are accumulated in the intestine until they are sufficiently concentrated. Then they are absorbed into the blood stream which carries them through the portal vein to the liver.

In the liver, the simple sugar is converted into glycogen by pancreatic enzymes. The carbohydrates can be stored as fat or disposed of as energy. The liver regulates a cycle in which it releases glycogen to the blood stream. Some of this is carried to the muscles and stored

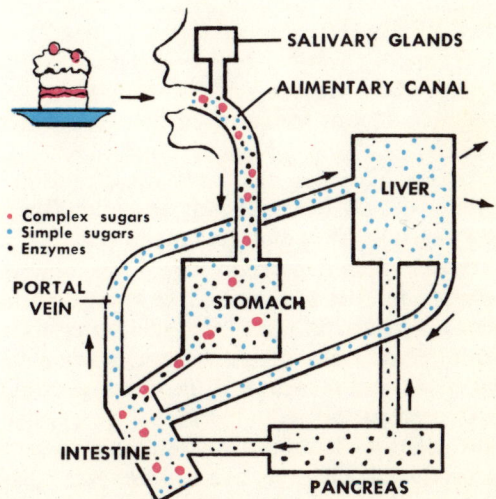

## ✳ THINGS TO DO

**COLLECTING CARBON FROM OXIDATION**

1 Hold a spoon or coin over the flame of a candle. Soon it will have a black deposit on it.
2 The candle is made of carbon and hydrogen. When a cold object is placed near it reduces the temperature preventing complete oxidation.
3 The carbon not burned collects on the spoon or coin.

If a diamond were to be burned at an extremely high temperature (2000° C), in the absence of air, it would be changed to GRAPHITE. Graphite is another crystalline form of carbon, and unlike the diamond, is a very soft substance. When mixed with clay and baked, it becomes the "lead" of lead pencils. Non-crystalline carbon is called *amorphous* (without definite form).

Other impure forms of carbon exist, such as COAL, coke, lampblack, bone black and charcoal. Coal has many varieties, each differing from the others largely as to the degree of CARBONIZATION that has taken place. The varieties such as anthracite, bituminous, lignite and peat are used as fuels and as the starting point for other organic compounds. COKE is the main product formed when bituminous coal is heated in the absence of air. It is used in the manufacture of gases, carbon compounds, and as a fuel. LAMPBLACK is produced when carbon compounds, oils, or natural gas are burned in the absence of

sufficient air for complete combustion, and the smoky gas flame is then chilled. The very finely divided black carbon, also called *carbon black* or *soot,* is used in large quantities in manufacturing printer's ink, phonograph records, and as a black pigment for shoe polish, black paints, and carbon paper. It is also used as a filler in rubber tires, greatly increasing their strength. Bone black, or animal charcoal, is produced when animal bones undergo destructive DISTILLATION. It is only about 15 per cent carbon, but because it is so porous, it absorbs large quantities of gases and coloring matter from solutions. It is used extensively in sugar refining to remove color, and to remove color and odors from drinking water. CHARCOAL results from the destructive distillation of wood. Activated charcoal, prepared from coconut shells, wood or coal, is used in gas masks as it adsorbs most poisonous gases. It also is used in sugar refining and in the purification of solvents. It serves the same purpose as coke, when the latter is not available, in the reduction of metals, and as a household fuel.

Carbon, with chemical symbol C, is found in all living tissues, combined with hydrogen, oxygen and nitrogen. The energy of both plant and animal life is derived from the OXIDATION of carbon compounds, such as the sugars and starches in the body. Carbon gives man food and clothing, since it is the basis upon which all animal and vegetable tissues are built. Green grass, hay, honey and starch all contain carbon. It is present in tea, coffee, bread, vinegar, butter, and almost every other article of food. Cotton and wool contain much carbon. Carbon provides most of man's FUEL. In coal, kerosene, oil, fat, lard, suet, blubber, or wood, carbon is one of the elements which unites with oxygen, giving off heat and light.

Carbon is so important that the some eight hundred thousand carbon compounds are studied as a separate branch of chemistry, called *organic chemistry*. Within this branch, many compounds have been synthesized in the laboratory to form important drugs, dyes, and plastics. Beside these compounds, there is a considerable quantity of mineral CARBONATES distributed throughout the earth. They have many industrial applications.      D. L. D.

SEE ALSO: CARBON CYCLE, CARBON LIFE, HYDROCARBON, ORGANIC COMPOUNDS

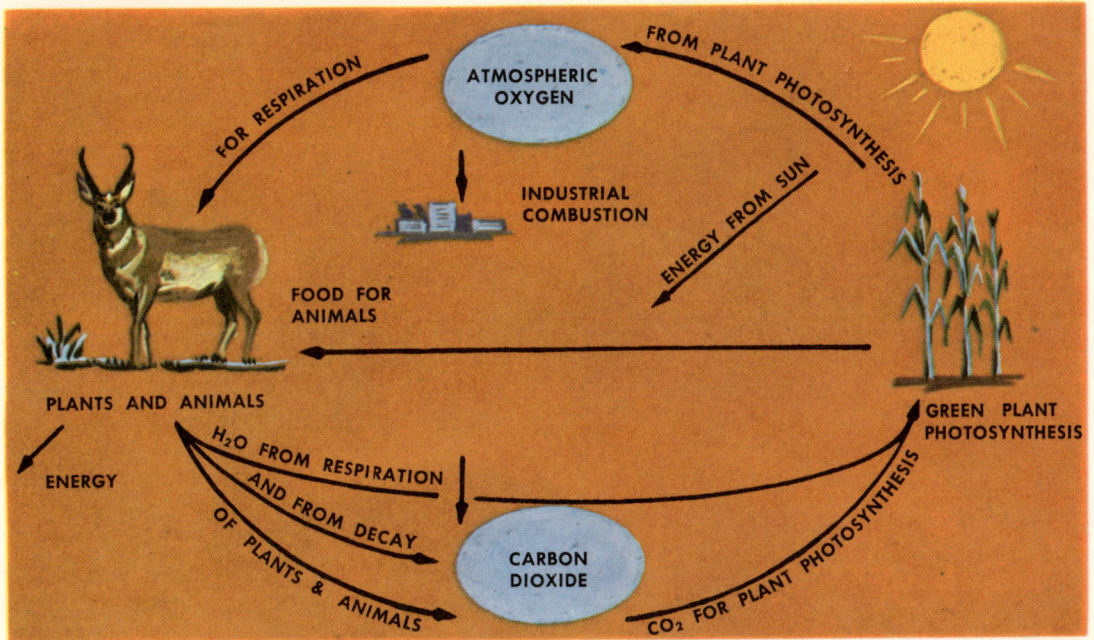

**Carbon cycle** The carbon cycle is nature's way of adjusting the amounts of carbon and oxygen, so that both ELEMENTS will remain in proper balance. Humans need oxygen to breathe, and they exhale CARBON DIOXIDE, a carbon compound, as a waste product. Green plants, on the other hand, need carbon dioxide in order to make food, but they release OXYGEN as their waste product. If the processes which require oxygen from the atmosphere continued indefinitely without other processes to absorb the carbon dioxide—the waste product of these reactions—the atmosphere would be so heavily concentrated with carbon dioxide that it would no longer be habitable.

The cycle described above is a very incomplete one. Actually, much more is involved beside PHOTOSYNTHESIS and respiration. Carbon dioxide is returned to the atmosphere whenever organic substances are consumed—whether it be by fire, by body energy, or by decay. This encompasses many processes. When coal or wood are consumed by fire, carbon dioxide is produced. When men or animals consume the food-fuel of their bodies, carbon dioxide is exhaled and excreted. Decay of both plant and animal life after death produces carbon dioxide. The process of FERMENTATION supplies carbon dioxide, and the same gas issues from volcanoes and from the soil in regions which are no longer volcanic.

Plants utilize carbon dioxide from the air and water absorbed by their roots. With the sun's energy and the green pigment, CHLOROPHYLL, a chemical reaction results to form a carbohydrate, out of which the plant builds its own body. The waste product, oxygen, is released. Thus, the sun's energy is stored in the plant. Some of the carbon dioxide in the atmosphere goes into the waters of the ocean. This is used by water animals in the building of shells (calcium carbonate).

The materials of the plant bodies are eaten by men and animals and so built into human and animal tissue. Whenever man consumes any part of a plant, the energy stored in that carbohydrate is now able to work for him in active living. With this energy release, carbon dioxide is formed again—and the entire cycle repeats. Some carbon compounds are not readily attacked by animals and microorganisms, and a slight but steady loss of carbon to sediments has produced an accumulation of COAL and PETROLEUM products. However, once these products are burned, carbon dioxide is again formed, keeping the balance intact. D. L. D.
SEE ALSO: BALANCE OF NATURE, CARBON LIFE

---

\* **THINGS TO DO**

### HOW CAN CARBON DIOXIDE BE PRODUCED?

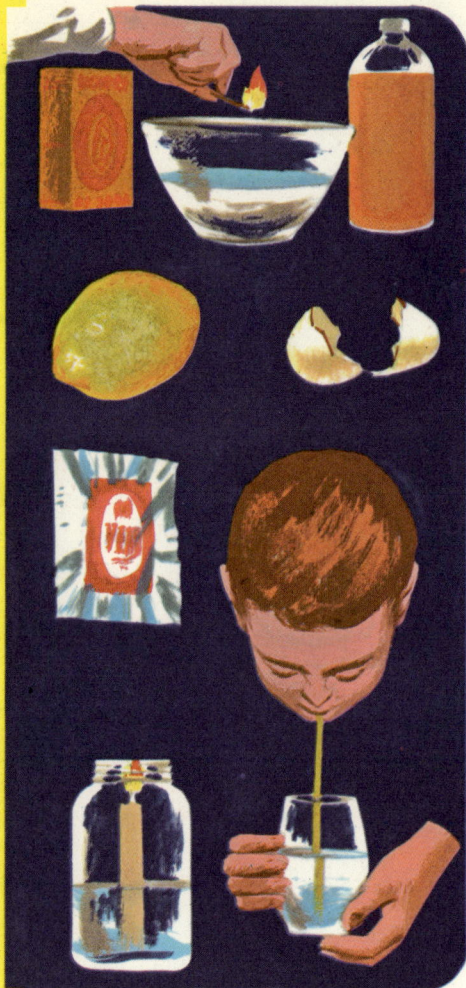

Accepting the fact that fire will not burn in air which is highly concentrated with carbon dioxide, one can test the combination of two materials which release carbon dioxide.

1   Combine baking soda and vinegar in a cup. Light a match and hold it over the solution. The flame will be extinguished.

2   Repeat the experiment above substituting lemon juice and either lime chips, chalk, or egg shells for the two materials to be combined.

3   Mix yeast in warm sugar water. This plant feeds on the sugar releasing carbon dioxide and alcohol. Hold a lighted match over the mixture to test for this release.

4   Lime water becomes cloudy when combined with carbon dioxide. Using a straw, blow air into a glass of lime-water. Notice the color before and after. We exhale carbon dioxide.

5   Burning will produce carbon dioxide. Burn a candle which has been placed in a jar with a small amount of lime-water. After several minutes extinguish the flame, cover the jar, and shake lightly. The limewater becomes cloudy.

**Carbon dioxide** Carbon dioxide is a colorless, tasteless gas, widely distributed in nature. It is a vital part of the CARBON CYCLE. Carbon dioxide is obtained from natural wells, from direct manufacture, and from chemical processes as a by-product as in the fermentation of grain.

Carbon dioxide has a large assortment of uses. As a solid, called "DRY ICE," it is a better refrigerant than ice because it evaporates directly to a gas and has an extremely low temperature, making it particularly useful in frozen food industries and in preservation of perishables. Liquid carbon dioxide, which has a blanketing effect on fire and reduces the temperature below the ignition point, is used extensively in FIRE EXTINGUISHERS. Carbonated beverages (soda water) provide a big market for carbon dioxide. It gives "bite" to the drink by forming the weak carbonic acid. As a pressure medium for instantaneous inflation, small carbon dioxide cartridges are packaged with life rafts and preservers. Carbon dioxide is used chemically in leavening agents, such as baking powder, and in neutralizing water in water-softening plants. Manufacturing paint, electric arc welding, and commercially preparing and packaging foods all require the use of carbon dioxide.    D. L. D.

**Carbon life** Modern science recognizes that all forms of life must be based on certain chemical processes. The term "chemical process" means a reaction or sequence of reactions of atoms or molecules. In the course of the chemical process, heat is either generated or absorbed.

Simple chemical reactions are the burning of HYDROGEN ($H_2$) and OXYGEN ($O_2$) to water ($H_2O$), or the burning of CARBON (C) in oxygen to form CARBON DIOXIDE ($CO_2$) or else CARBON MONOXIDE (CO) if the combustion is not complete. In both cases, heat is generated by taking elements (such as the atom C or the molecules $H_2$, $O_2$) and combining them to form COMPOUNDS. Compounds are combinations of two or more elements. Therefore, they almost always consist of bigger and more complex molecules than the ELEMENTS.

Lifeless (inorganic) compounds consist of relatively small molecules, mostly containing far less than 100 atoms. The reason for this is that most elements are "choosey," that is, they combine only with a small number of other elements. The two major exceptions are the elements SILICON and carbon. The *affinity* (willingness to form compounds with other elements) of carbon by far exceeds that of silicon.

Life substances (ORGANIC COMPOUNDS) consist of very large, complex molecules, containing many hundreds and even thousands of atoms and a great number of elements, although they are mostly carbon and hydrogen. Of these two, carbon forms the basic structure of the large organic molecules. This applies to all forms of life on Earth and, therefore, they are often referred to as *carbon life*.

The strength of carbon has two advantages. Firstly, it lends great stability to the large organic molecules. Secondly, carbon's affinity to other elements helps in preventing slow poisoning of living organisms. A POISON is a chemical substance which for some reason is incompatible with the organic substance or with the functioning of a living organism. If a poison, however, is consumed in very small quantities, it may not be effective (harmful).

Under everyday conditions, tiny quantities of poison enter living organisms all the time. If permitted to accumulate, they could be deadly. Actually, they are either discharged or chemically destroyed, because the affinity of carbon breaks the bonds which hold the hostile molecules together, thereby rendering the substance harmless.

Technically speaking, all living organisms are little heat engines. If enough people or animals fill a cold room, it soon becomes noticeably warmer. Moving organisms (animals and man) especially need energy which is generated by the combustion of food in the body. The required oxygen enters the blood through the lungs, combustion products are discharged through the bowels (solid), through the kidneys and skin pores (liquid) and through the lungs (gaseous, such as $CO_2$ and water vapor). Thus, animals consume oxygen. Land animals take oxygen out of the air, sea animals take it out of the water. Land animals would suffocate within minutes in an atmosphere which contains no oxygen, sea animals would similarly suffocate in a fluid which contains no oxygen, for instance, in a sea of oil.

Plants, the other principal form of earth life, are generally thought of as generating, but not consuming, oxygen. It is, however, more correct to say that plants do not require free oxygen like land animals do. Plants can absorb $CO_2$, break it apart and thereby set the oxygen free. They do need a small quantity of $O_2$ for their own respiration. Most of it they discharge into the atmosphere and thereby make it "breathable" for the animals. Thus, plants and animals complement each other; plants discharge free oxygen and animals discharge $CO_2$. The life of animals depends on plants; but, since there are many sources of $CO_2$ (for example, volcanoes), plants do not need animals for their existence.

History of life on this planet indicates

indeed that plants were the first forms of life to inhabit the oceans and the first to conquer the land. Since the earth's ATMOSPHERE contains a much higher percentage of free oxygen than the atmospheres of other planets, one may suspect that this is the result of plants decomposing $CO_2$ and discharging the $O_2$ into the atmosphere for many millions of years (while the carbon finally became coal). Not until the plants made the air breathable, could carbon life develop outside the oceans.     K. A. E.

SEE ALSO: SILICON LIFE

**Carbon monoxide** Carbon monoxide is a colorless, poisonous, odorless gas. It is formed by burning carbon with an insufficient supply of air.

The gas, chemical formula CO, is important in metallurgy for separating a metal from its ore—especially in the extraction of iron in the blast furnace, and for refining nickel. Carbon monoxide has great application in the synthetic organic chemistry field for industrial uses. It is extensively used as a fuel gas.

Because it is odorless, caution must be used when the deadly gas is present. Car engines running in closed garages or leaky furnaces present the greatest dangers.

If a person inhales carbon monoxide, it gets into the BLOOD. When this happens there is no room in the red cells for the oxygen needed by body tissues.     D. L. D.

**Carbon star** see Star

**Carbon tetrachloride** (tet-trah-KLO-ride) Carbon tetrachloride is a colorless, pleasant-smelling, non-flammable liquid which is composed of carbon and chlorine. It is manufactured by chemical reaction.

It is an excellent solvent for fats, greases, waxes, and other organic compounds. It has a large commercial use as a dry-cleaning fluid and spot-remover. Carbon tetrachloride, chemical formula $CCl_4$, is used in "pyrene" FIRE EXTINGUISHERS because its dense vapors exclude air from the fire, and it rapidly absorbs heat. It is used particularly for oil and electrical fires. It is also used in the manufacture of freon refrigerants. Its fumes are toxic and should not be inhaled.     D. L. D.

✳ **THINGS TO DO**

**WILL CARBON TETRACHLORIDE PUT OUT FIRE?**

**Materials: atomizer, such as used for perfumes; pan, cookie sheet, carbon tetrachloride (cleaning fluid—read directions on can)**

**Because the fumes are poisonous, this experiment MUST be done out of doors.**

1   Fill an atomizer half full of carbon tetrachloride. Place it in a pan of hot water. Gas from the chemical is quickly formed.

2   Crumple up newspaper, place it on a cookie sheet, and set it on fire.

3   Squirt the atomizer over the flames. The fire goes out.

4   Carbon tetrachloride is heavier than air, does not burn, and does not support combustion.

**Carbonates** Carbonates are COM-POUNDS in which a metal combines with a special grouping of one part carbon to three parts oxygen, known as the carbonate ion ($CO_3^{--}$), to form a salt. Carbonic acid ($H_2CO_3$), the familiar "soda water," contains this carbonate ion. It is sometimes used commercially in a chemical reaction to produce a desired carbonate. Carbonates are found widely distributed in nature. For example, CALCIUM CAR-BONATE ($CaCO_3$) exists as CALCITE, marble, limestone, and in fish shells. The common rock, DOLOMITE, is a double carbonate of magnesium and calcium [$CaMg(CO_3)_2$].

Sodium carbonate ($Na_2CO_3$), commonly known as washing soda, is used in the manufacture of glass, paper, and textiles, and is a household cleaning agent. Basic lead carbonate $Pb_3(OH_2)(CO_3)_2$, known as *white lead,* is still the most important PAINT base. Carbonates of iron, called *siderite* ($FeCO_3$); of manganese, called *rhodochrosite* ($MnCO_3$); of magnesium, called *magnesite* ($MgCO_3$); and of zinc, called *smithsonite* ($ZnCO_3$) are all common. Many others exist, too.

Carbonates are insoluble in water, except those of sodium, potassium, and ammonium. When heated, carbonates break down to their oxides and carbon dioxide. The carbonates can be converted into bicarbonates by adding excess carbon dioxide. One example is sodium bicarbonate ($NaHCO_3$), known as baking soda.                D. L. D.

SEE ALSO: SODIUM BICARBONATE

**Carbonic acid** see Acids and bases

**Carboniferous age** see Geologic time table

**Carbonization** The term *carbonization* generally refers to three processes. Since these processes are somewhat different, it is best to discuss each process individually.

(1) The most common usage of the term involves transforming organic matter into CHARCOAL, a residue of carbon, by fire or a corrosive chemical. The distillation of COAL is the heating of bituminous coal in the absence of air to obtain coke and other valuable by-products.

The temperature of carbonization determines which by-products will result. High-temperature carbonization of coal (1000–1300° C) yields AMMONIA, fuel gas, light oil, and COAL TAR as by-products of coke. Low-temperature carbonization (400–750° C) produces by-products of PETRO-LEUM, gas, and large amounts of coal tar and liquids.

(2) Carbonization also refers to a textile process of removing vegetable matter from wool. The matter may be burrs, bark, grass and cotton fibers. These organic impurities are destroyed by acids or salts, reduced to carbon, and removed by mechanical means.

(3) An entirely different process—that of combining, covering, or impregnating a substance with carbon is still another definition of carbonization. An example of this process is the "cementation" process for making STEEL.                D. L. D.

**Carburetor** (KAHR-buh-ray-ter) A carburetor is an apparatus in which air or gas is mixed with carbon compounds which can easily turn into vapor. This mixture of gas and carbon compounds can produce more energy than can the gas or carbon alone. In an AUTOMOBILE carburetor, air is mixed with gasoline spray (a carbon compound) to produce an easily exploded mixture.

SEE: ENGINES

**Carcinoma** see Cancer (disease)

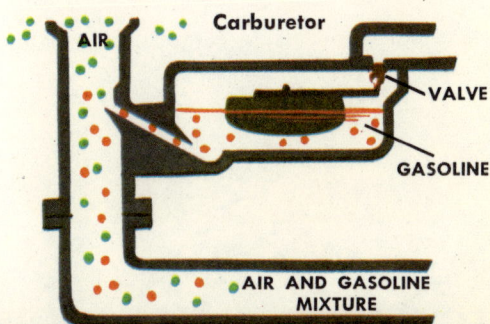

AIR · Carburetor · VALVE · GASOLINE · AIR AND GASOLINE MIXTURE

**Cardamom** (KAHR-duh-mum) The cardamom plant is grown for the seed which comes from the pod of the dried fruit. The tall plant, native to India, grows from eight to twelve feet high and is cultivated commercially.

The tiny, whole cardamom seeds are used in pickling spices, curry powder blends and other prepared spice seasonings. The whole seed as well as the ground cardamom is a favorite with some people for use in sweet pastries and cookies. This exotic HERB adds interesting flavor to bread, rolls, cookies, gelatins and jellies. The cardamom seed gives an oil which is used medicinally as a stimulant.       J. K. K.

SEE ALSO: GINGER

**Cardinal** The cardinal is often called a *redbird*. It has a cheery song which sounds like a boy whistling for his dog. The male has beautiful red feathers, and the female has a duller, gray-red coat. On its head the BIRD has a crest of feathers like a peaked cap. Both the female and the male have bright red bills. Adult birds are about eight inches long.

Cardinals usually live in the eastern United States, from New York to the Gulf of Mexico. They sometimes range as far north as southern Canada and as far west as the Mississippi River.

Their nests, composed of dead leaves, grass, and weed stems, are usually found in low trees or thickets of brush. Cardinals lay three to five eggs and usually have two broods of young in a mating season.

Their chief sources of food are weeds and fruit seeds, but they will eat insects. Their strong, wide bills are ideal for cracking seeds.       V. V. N.

**A male cardinal**
Mrs. Allen D. Cruickshank

**Cardinal climber**

**Cardinal climber** The cardinal climber is a VINE belonging to the MORNING-GLORY family. The two inch flowers are red on the outside and white inside.

These vines grow from seeds planted indoors during the early spring. After all danger of frost is past, the young seedlings may be transplanted into the garden. Cardinal climbers grow on fences, screens, and trellises.       M. R. L.

SEE ALSO: TRANSPLANTING

**Cardiograph** see Electrocardiograph

**Cardiovascular system** see Circulatory system

**Caribou** see Deer family

**Caries** see Tooth decay

**Carnation** (kar-NA-shun) The carnation is a flower that smells like cloves. It has ruffled, jagged-edged petals and usually comes in shades of pink, red, and white. The red carnation is the state flower of Ohio. Men have grown carnations for over 2,000 years.

Carnations belong to a group of flowers called PINKS. Originally they came from Europe, but many varieties are grown in the United States.

Carnations are most often grown in greenhouses, PROPAGATION being by cuttings. They have brittle stems and narrow grass-like leaves, and they grow to about three feet in height.       J. M. C.

**Carnation**

A carnivore skull (left) compared with the skull of a plant-eating animal

**Carnivore** (KAHR-nuh-vore) The cat, dog, bear, skunk and seal are among the three hundred different mammals called carnivores. These animals eat a great deal of meat, and that is why they are called *carni-* (flesh) *vore* (eating).

All carnivores have tails and long canine teeth. While some of these meat-eaters occasionally attack men, many are useful. The mink, sable, seal and ermine are valued as furs. The cat and raccoon kill mice and other rodents, and the cat and dog are commonly used as pets.

All animals of Order *Carnivora* eat meat, but there is considerable variety in the diet of different animals. Those carnivores with webbed feet, the seal, sea lion and walrus, are specially fitted for swimming and eat fish. The group with separate toes includes all other carnivores. The cat-like and dog-like animals are excellent hunters and often eat only meat. The bears, however, eat vegetables as well as meat in their diet. The skunk is particularly fond of eggs and meats while his relatives, the weasel and mink, often hunt just for the joy of killing. The raccoon eats everything from clams and fish to fruit and vegetables.

Carnivores have no single characteristic which separates them from all other mammals. They are classified on the basis of many physical features. Most have five toes on each foot, and none have fewer than four. Usually they have claws on their toes and two tufts of very sensitive whiskers (*vibrissae*) on their cheeks. They have six incisor teeth and two long canine teeth in both upper and lower jaws. Their cheek teeth are blade-like and snip past each other like scissors. Like man, carnivores have two sets of teeth in their lifetimes.     J. L. K.

**Carnotite** Carnotite is an important ore of URANIUM. It contains some radium. It is a yellow crystalline powder which occurs mainly in sandstone deposits in the western United States.

**Carotene** see Vitamin

**Carotid artery** see Circulatory system

Chicago Natural History Museum
**Carp**

**Carp** Carp is a type of fresh-water fish. A large minnow was brought to California from Asia in 1872. It is now found in inland lakes and streams throughout America. Carp sometimes grow to be three feet long and weigh 25 pounds. It has four *barbels* or feelers around the mouth.

The carp is useful because it can be eaten. But it is also harmful because it destroys eggs and breeding places of more valuable fish. A few kinds of carp are the scale carp which is completely scaled, the mirror carp with a few large scales, and the leather carp with no scales at all.     J. K. K.
SEE ALSO: FISH, PISCES

**Carpel** see Capsule

**Carrier wave** A carrier wave is a high frequency radio wave. Some characteristic of it is changed or modulated in accordance with another wave so that music or speech is transmitted.
SEE: RADIO, SOUND, TELEVISION

**Carriers** Carriers are individuals who carry DISEASE germs in their bodies and pass these germs to others even though the carriers themselves may never have the disease.

Civil Air Patrol
**A flat map of the earth's surface**

Carrot

**Carrot** The carrot is a plant with an orange ROOT that is eaten as a vegetable, either raw or cooked. The leaves of the carrot are fern-like and lacy. Carrots need two years to complete their life cycle (BIENNIALS).

Carrot seeds should be planted in well-drained, prepared soil, free of lumps and rocks. The young seedlings should be thinned so that the roots will grow straight and thick. The best root stock is produced when the temperature ranges from 60 to 75° F.

The ancient Greeks and Romans used carrots for medicines, not food. Although the early colonists grew carrots for food, Americans did not grow them in large quantities until 1920. The wild carrot is a weed. J. M. C.

**Cartilage tissue** (KAR-tuh-lij) Cartilage tissue is a pearly-white, firm, tough, and elastic animal tissue. The cartilage cells secrete this material sometimes called *gristle*. It is found between the bones of the body. Cartilage acts as a cushion between these bones. Many bony structures are not fully developed in babies. Cartilage is found in these undeveloped parts. Gradually the cartilage changes to BONE. Since cartilage contains little calcium, it is not regarded as a bone.

There are two basic types of cartilage. *Temporary cartilage* changes to bone in the early periods of life. At birth, the ends of the long bones in the body are temporary cartilage. By the end of approximately six months, this cartilage changes to bone.

*Permanent cartilage* is located at the joints of bones, in the nose, in the external ear, and is the foundation for the eyelids. Tubes of the RESPIRATORY SYSTEM, including the wind pipe and the larynx, contain permanent cartilage. In weight-bearing joints, such as the knee, cartilage is especially tough and elastic. The cartilage pads, located between each one of the vertebrae, cushion the body against shock. These pads also make it easier for the body to twist and to bend. P. F. D.

SEE ALSO: HISTOLOGY, SKELETON

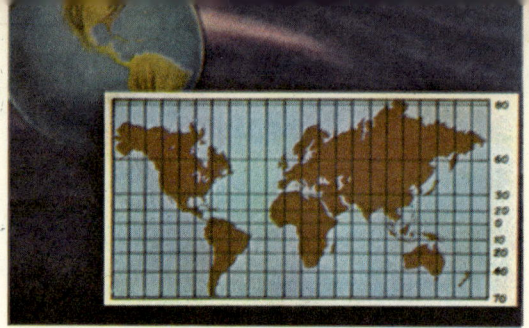

**Cartography** Cartography is the making of maps or charts for the purpose of picturing the earth's surface as seen from above.

Maps are drawn to scale. They are based on surveys, laid out from photographs or made from existing maps. First the projection is selected and the specifications drawn. Different types of lettering are used to distinguish political units, man-made features, water features and to indicate their size. Geological features are indicated by contour lines or by shading. Various symbols used are identified in a key. E. R. B.
SEE ALSO: MAP-MAKING, PROJECTION

**Carver, George Washington** (1864?–1943) Carver was an American agricultural chemist. Born in slavery, he lived to enjoy international fame. Forty-five years of his life he spent at Tuskegee Institute in Alabama working on new ways to help the South restore its land. The soil had been worn out by the continual growing of COTTON. Carver encouraged the planting of peanuts and sweet potatoes to nourish and restore the soil. Carver experimented in his laboratory and discovered over 300 uses of the peanut and more than 125 uses of the sweet potato.

Among the products that he made from peanuts were wood dyes, soap, shampoo, linoleum and metal polish, ink, cooking oils, peanut butter, and cheese. From the sweet potato he created such products as a valuable rubber compound, starch, imitation ginger, library paste, vinegar, wood filler, rope, and instant coffee.

About the time of the official emancipation of the slaves, George Washington Carver was born to slave parents on the farm of Moses Carver in Diamond Grove, Missouri. His father was killed shortly before his birth, and when he was about six months old, Night Raiders kidnapped him and his mother. No one knows what happened to the young mother, but the baby was returned to Moses Carver by a man who found the child abandoned on the road, desperately ill with whooping cough. This disease affected his voice so that it remained high and thin all his life.

Having had no children of their own, the Carvers were fond of young George. It was with regret that they allowed him to leave for school in Neosha, Missouri, but they realized that his keen mind craved satisfaction.

In Neosha, Carver found his first real happiness with Mariah Watkins, a large, motherly washer woman. She taught him how to wash and iron, a skill which later helped him earn money to pay for his college tuition. She gave him a Bible, which he kept in his possession no matter where he went for seventy years. He read the Bible eagerly, and he memorized the passages that had to do with the earth and growing things.

After Carver was graduated from Iowa State College at Ames with a Master's degree in agriculture, he continued to teach at the college. He received many invitations to teach in southern schools, but he considered none until Booker T. Washington asked him to come to Tuskegee Institute to teach, do research, and help the neighboring farmers reclaim their land. He found great satisfaction in his laboratory, for he was a quiet man who did not like crowds or public acclaim. When THOMAS A. EDISON offered him over $50,000 a year to work in his laboratory in California, Carver refused. Money meant nothing to him. He never accepted an increase in salary at Tuskegee, and he often did not cash the salary checks he did receive. He never applied for a patent on his discoveries because he said, "God gave them to me. Why should I claim them for my own?" D. H. J.

**Casein** see Dairy products, Paints

**Cashew** see Nuts

**Cassia** see Cinnamon

Cassiopeia

**Cassiopeia** (kass-ee-uh-PEE-uh) Cassiopeia is a group of stars that looks like a W or an M in the sky. Ancient people thought it looked like a chair or a woman in a chair. Cassiopeia is near POLARIS, the North Star. In the northern part of the world it can be seen on most nights of the year.

Cassiopeia was the name of the wife of CEPHEUS, who was king of Ethiopia. They had a daughter named Andromeda. The three members of this royal family are all immortalized in constellations. Cassiopeia was a very beautiful woman. She was also vain. She boasted that she was more beautiful than the sea nymphs. The sea nymphs were insulted and they complained to the god of the sea, Neptune. Neptune decided to punish Cassiopeia by having a terrible monster attack the coast of Ethiopia. Cepheus went to the oracle of Jupiter to find out how to get rid of the monster. The oracle told him that he would have to sacrifice his daughter Andromeda to the monster. Cepheus chained Andromeda to a rock along the shore for the monster. Andromeda was saved by Perseus, who is also immortalized in a constellation.

Some legends say that the sea nymphs were angry when Cassiopeia was given a place in the sky. They asked Jupiter to arrange it so that she would hang upside down part of the night.                C. L. K.

SEE ALSO: CONSTELLATIONS

**Cassiterite** see Tin

**Cast iron** see Iron

**Castor oil**  Castor oil is made from the seeds, or "castor beans," of the castor-oil plant. It is used in making soaps and paint, for engine oil and as a medicine acting as an irritant in the intestinal tract.

A

B

A—Cat's eyes at night
B—In daylight, iris narrows

Claws sheathed

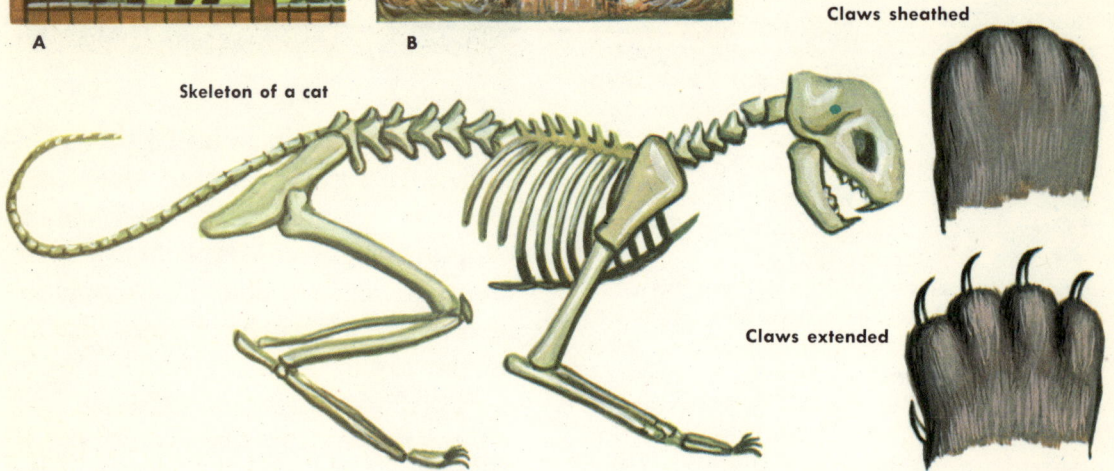

Skeleton of a cat

Claws extended

**Cat family** All cats, from small, gentle house cats to wild lions and tigers, belong to the same animal family. There are about forty different kinds (species) of cats.

Cats are among the best hunters of the flesh-eating animals (CARNIVORES). The *saber-toothed tiger,* which lived long ago, had a pair of upper teeth eight inches long which looked like daggers. It used these dagger-like teeth to kill wild horses, camels, and other animals much larger than itself, Although cats today do not have dagger-like teeth, they are well-equipped for the task of hunting.

CHARACTERISTICS OF CATS

All cats have long, curved CLAWS, with which they can grip and tear the flesh of their prey. They keep these claws sharp by scraping them on tree trunks or other rough surfaces. People who own house cats often give them wooden scratching posts. Most cats' claws can be pulled back (retracted) into folds of skin (*sheaths*) at the ends of their toes. When its claws are retracted, a cat can walk silently.

Cats walk on their toes; their heel bones do not touch the ground. They have five toes on each front foot and four on each back foot. Small pads on their feet cushion their walk and help them to move quietly.

Most cats hunt at night. They are helped by a fairly good sense of smell, keen hearing, and the ability to see very well in dim light. The cells within a cat's eye are very sensitive to light. At night, the colored part (iris) of a cat's eye opens exceptionally wide, letting in extra light and enabling the cat to see better than most other animals. In the day, the iris closes to a thin vertical slit, shutting out the bright light. This is true of cats that hunt at night. Those that hunt during the day, such as the lion and the cheetah, have irises which contract into small circles like those of humans and other animals.

A cat is a graceful animal with excellent control over the muscles of its body. It has over five hundred muscles which it can control and use at will. Its backbone is flexible so it can twist and turn easily. It can climb well and balance itself easily. It can run swiftly for short distances and take great and powerful leaps. After stalking its prey, it leaps, knocks it down, and then bites, tears, or shakes it to death.

Most wild members of the cat family are the color of the dry grass, dead leaves, and bare rock which make up the environment in which they live. They usually have from two to five cubs every other year.

The small cats kept as pets in people's homes are called *house cats*. Cats are not usually as friendly as dogs, and very few can be trained to do tricks and obey orders. However, they are neat, quiet and graceful pets and need less care than dogs. There are two kinds of house cats, shorthair and longhair. Siamese, manx, and stray or alley cats have short hair. Persian cats have long hair. They have heavier bodies than shorthair cats and long, silky coats which grow in great ruffs around their necks. Their toes and ears often have tufts of fur.

Cats shed their coats every spring, summer, and fall and shed their claws at various times during the year. The purring sounds that most cats make when relaxed are from a pair of false "vocal cords" above the true cords. The true cords relax and air is free to vibrate around the membranes of the false cords.

House cats have from four to eight kittens at one time and may have litters as often as two or three times a year. Pet cats should be given a warm, dry box for sleeping and two or three meals each day. Cats keep themselves clean with their rough tongues.

Cats have from thirty to thirty-two teeth, all of which are designed chiefly for cutting and tearing flesh. Flesh is more easily digested than grains and grasses, so the digestive system of the cat is rather simple in comparison with that of a cow or horse.

Cats' eyes glow in the dark because the cells of the retina are coated with a chemical (guanin) which reflects light.

The tabby is distinguished by its beautifully striped hair

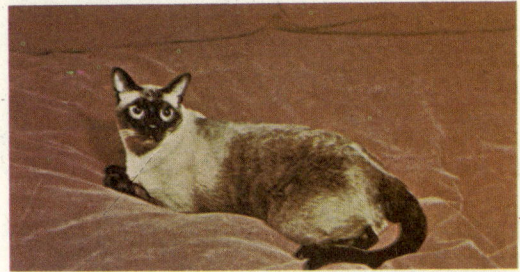

Courtesy Society For Visual Education, Inc.

The color in a Siamese cat's hair starts to appear several days after birth

The manx (originally from the Isle of Man) has no tail

F. A. Blashfield

The black, long-haired Angora has eyes that contrast sharply with the hair color

Chicago Natural History Museum

**Tigers hunt deer, water buffaloes, and young elephants in the jungles and grasslands of Asia**

### KINDS OF CATS

The earliest ancestor of the cat was the *miacis,* which lived over fifty-five million years ago. The miacis had a long body and tail, short legs, and looked somewhat like a weasel. It gradually developed into an animal that looked like the CIVET, a flesh-eating mammal found in warm areas of Africa and southern Asia. Cats as known today probably appeared on earth about forty million years ago.

The *cheetah,* also called the *hunting leopard,* is found in the open country of Africa and Asia. It is about six feet long and has a rough coat of fairly long, black-spotted yellow fur. Its claws are more blunt than those of other cats and may not be retracted. The cheetah hunts in the day and is often trained to hunt for man. Known as the world's fastest mammal, it can run up to seventy miles an hour over short distances. It runs down its prey instead of leaping upon it. Cheetahs hunt deer, antelope, goats, and fowl.

The *puma,* also called the *cougar, mountain lion, panther, painter, catamount,* and *kingcat,* is a large wild, sandy-colored cat about six feet long and weighs up to one hundred pounds. At one time pumas were found in all parts of North America, but now they are found mainly in Florida, the Blue Ridge Mountains, and the wilder parts of western United States. The puma is an excellent climber and can get up into the lower branches of trees with one graceful leap. It hunts and eats elk, deer, mountain beaver, porcupine, rodents, and sometimes cattle and horses. When it is finished eating, it will often cover remaining parts of its prey with sticks and leaves and save it for another day.

The *jaguar* is a wild member of the cat family found mainly in the jungles of Central and South America. It looks very much like a leopard but is heavier and has spots with black rings around them. Jaguars climb well and spend much of their time in trees, hunting birds and monkeys. They also hunt deer, fish, turtles, alligators, and sometimes cattle and horses. Jaguars don't hunt out in the open. They jump on their prey from a hiding place.

The *leopard,* also called a *panther,* is found in Africa, Asia, and parts of Europe. It has a tan coat covered with black spots usually arranged in small groups of five or six. The fur is valuable for coats. Some leopards have so many dark spots that they look as if they have black coats. Leopards are about seven feet long and weigh 125 pounds. They hunt monkeys, large birds, antelopes, jackals, and snakes. They are

All photos Courtesy Society For Visual Education, Inc.

Some wild members of the cat family: (from left—top) puma, black leopard; (center) ocelot, male lion, jaguarundi; (bottom) snow leopard, bobcat

very strong and often leap up into trees with prey weighing as much as eighty pounds.

The *lion,* the "king of beasts," lives in the grasslands and sandy plains of India and Africa. It has yellowish-brown fur, is eight to ten feet long, and weighs about four hundred pounds. The male lion has a huge mane and a bush-tipped tail. Lions hunt alone or in small groups (*prides*). Their prey includes zebras, young elephants, antelopes, and sometimes domestic animals. A lion can break the neck of its prey with one blow of its powerful forelegs. Young lions in the circus are taught simple tricks, but they never become really tame.

The Canadian *lynx,* sometimes called a *wildcat* or *true lynx,* has long, silky, brownish-gray fur, a stumpy tail, and tufted ears. It lives in forests and rocky areas of Canada. The soles of its large feet are furred in winter and serve as snowshoes, making it possible for the lynx to walk on the top of the snow. It hunts at night for mice, squirrels, foxes, birds, and hares, especially the snowshoe hare.

The *bay lynx,* or *bobcat,* is smaller than the wildcat. A more southerly animal, it is found in the rocky areas of the United States. It has brownish-gray fur with black spots and a short bobbed tail from which

it gets its name. Bobcats prey on wood rats, mice, rabbits, muskrats, squirrels, and sometimes deer and sheep.

The *ocelot* looks like a very big house cat. It is about fifty inches long, weighs thirty pounds, and has gray and tan fur marked in definite patterns of spots and stripes. This beautiful cat lives in the forests of Central and South America. Ocelots hunt and eat lizards, monkeys, snakes, birds, rabbits, rats, mice, sheep, and pigs. They are the most gentle of the wild cats and are often tamed and kept as house pets.

*Tigers* are very large cats with yellow fur and black stripes. They are about eight to ten feet long and weigh as much as four hundred pounds. They are found in the jungle and grasslands of Asia. Tigers hunt by night for deer, antelope, water buffalo, and young elephants. They kill not only for food but also for the love of blood. Tigers have been known to kill people when other food has been scarce. They are excellent swimmers and good climbers.

Other wild members of the cat family include: the caracal, European wildcat, golden cat, jaguarundi, margay, ounce, palla's cat, and the serval.                     D. J. A.

# Catabolism see Metabolism

Catalpa

**Catalpa** (kuh-TAL-puh) The catalpa is a tall, stately shade tree much used in parks and gardens for its beauty. It is often called the *Indian bean tree* because its seeds grow in long narrow pods like giant string beans.

Catalpa trees grow in the United States, the West Indies, and China. They belong to the *bignonia* or *trumpet-creeper* family.

The tree has a short trunk and a broad dome-topped pyramidal shape. It grows to sixty feet in height.

The leaves are heart-shaped with a fuzzy underside. The flowers which grow in pointed clusters, are bell-shaped and are white streaked with brown. The bark is thin, scaly, and furrowed. The wood is dark brown and soft but very durable, often being used for fence posts because it does not rot readily.

Pests that attack the catalpa are the catalpa midge, the catalpa sphinx caterpillar, and the mealy bug.          J. M. C.

**Catalyst** (KAT-uh-list) A catalyst, or *catalytic agent,* is a substance which alters the rate of speed of a chemical reaction without itself being permanently changed or appearing in the end product. Normally a catalyst hastens or encourages the rate of reaction. However, at times catalysts are used to slow down a reaction, particularly if decomposition is occurring too rapidly.

Catalysts are called *positive* or *negative,* depending on whether they *speed* up or *slow* down a chemical reaction.

Catalysis plays an important part in industrial chemistry. A great number of chemicals are produced by catalytic processes. Platinum, for example, is a valuable commercial catalyst, used in many reactions. Platinum powder or platinized asbestos is used in the preparation of sulfuric acid. Platinum gauze is used in preparing nitric acid. Zinc oxide and copper (or other catalysts) are used in manufacturing methanol. Thousands of catalysts exist. Even water is one. Catalysts in living systems are called ENZYMES. Bacteria and molds are used in industry as biological catalysts.

Catalysts are used in two different situations: (1) to increase a rate already detectable without a catalyst, and (2) to encourage the substances reacting to form several different products (only one or none of which would occur at detectable rates without a catalyst). In this second situation, the choice that is made as to which product (or products) should be formed is called *selectivity.* For example, when carbon monoxide and hydrogen react under carefully controlled temperature and pressure conditions, the variation of catalysts produces varied results. With nickel as a catalyst, the result is methane and water. With cobalt and thorium dioxide as catalysts, the main products are methane, ethane, propane, butane, pentane, water and others. Other catalysts produce still more products.

The catalyst may be in the same physical state as the substances reacting (*homogeneous* catalysis), or in a different state (*heterogeneous* catalysis).          D. L. D.

## ✳ THINGS TO DO

### CAN A CHEMICAL CHANGE BE SPEEDED UP?

1　Wearing an insulated glove, hold a tablespoon of sugar over a flame. Permit it to burn. It will melt and turn brown but will not blaze up.

2　Repeat the experiment, only this time mix ashes in the sugar. Now the sugar will burn freely.

3　The ash is a catalyst to hasten oxidation but does not change in form as the sugar does.

**Cataract** (KATT-uh-rackt) Cataract is a disease affecting the lens of the EYE. The lens consists of a semi-solid substance enclosed in a capsule. In the normal, healthy eye the lens is transparent. Cataract is a condition in which the lens loses its transparency and tends to become opaque.

Cataracts are classified mainly as developmental or degenerative. *Developmental* cataract occurs while the lens is growing. The opacity may be caused by heredity, malnutrition, or inflammation. *Degenerative* cataracts occur in normally developed lenses and are usually associated with aging. Those associated with aging are called *senile* cataracts. Degenerative cataracts may also result from causes such as exposure of the lens to heat rays, radiation, or poisons as well as from disease.

Cataract may occur in only one eye or in both eyes. It may affect only the capsule or only the lens proper. It may affect both. The degree to which vision is impaired depends upon the parts of the lens affected and the area in which opacity occurs.

There is no medication known which can restore transparency to the lens. When vision is impaired by cataract the only method of treatment is surgery.　　　G. A. D.

SEE ALSO: OPTOMETRY

**Catbird** The catbird is about nine inches long and is colored slate gray. It has a reddish-brown patch under its tail feathers, and on the top of its head is a black cap. It may sing for hours on a warm, moonlit summer night.

The catbird can imitate the songs of other birds almost as well as the MOCKINGBIRD. It loves to visit gardens and many times builds its nest in shrubbery near houses.

It is related to the MOCKINGBIRD and spends most of the summer season in the northern United States and southern Canada. It flies south in the winter to the Gulf states, Cuba, Mexico, and Central America.

Catbirds are helpful because they are insectivorous. They feed on many harmful varieties of insects, such as beetles, ants, and crickets. They also eat wild and cultivated fruits including strawberries, raspberries, blackberries, and cherries.　V. V. N.

**Catbird**

Mrs. Allan D. Cruickshank

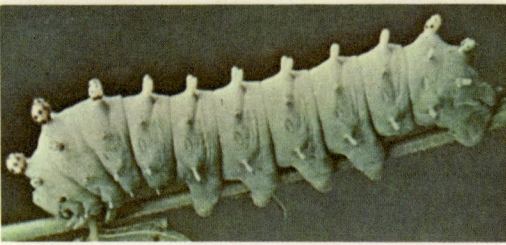

Courtesy Society For Visual Education, Inc.

**A common caterpillar**

**Cathode ray**

**Caterpillar** A caterpillar is the larva of a butterfly or MOTH. It looks like a worm. BUTTERFLIES and moths deposit eggs on or near a plant which is to be the food supply for the young caterpillar. Usually the eggs are deposited in the spring and develop into caterpillars during the summer.

The eggs do not hatch into forms anything like the adults. Instead, they produce worm-like caterpillars or larvae. All have several extra pairs of legs and biting mouth parts.

The caterpillar has a ravenous appetite, grows big and fat, and molts several times. The caterpillar does a great deal of damage to crops. Eventually it goes into a resting stage and becomes a pupa, emerging later as an adult moth or butterfly.     V. V. N.

SEE ALSO: LARVA, METAMORPHOSIS

**Catfish** Catfish is a large group of fish with long feelers (*barbels*) which look a little like cat's whiskers. They have sharp spines on the front of their back (dorsal) and breast (pectoral) fins. Sometimes these spines are poisonous. Catfish have no scales.

Catfish are fresh-water fish. They live near the muddy bottom of lakes, rivers, ponds and streams. Their long feelers move all the time, searching for food. Catfish eat both dead and living things. They also eat the waste from fish and water animals.

There are over a thousand different kinds of catfish. Some, such as blue catfish are very big, weighing over one hundred pounds. Others are so tiny they can be raised in an aquarium with goldfish or other small fish. Many catfish are good to eat.     D: J. A.

**Channel catfish**

Chicago Natural History Museum

**Cathode** A cathode is a negatively charged terminal point of an electrical circuit. In ELECTROLYSIS, the conductors that dip into the solution are called ELECTRODES, instead of terminals. The cathode is the negative electrode whereby the current enters the solution. The cathode's counterpart is the positively charged ANODE where the current leaves the solution and electrons enter the wires, to flow back to the cathode.

Similarly, electron tubes contain a small metal cathode which accepts electrons from the circuit. It in turn emits an electron stream to the anode in order to conduct the electrical current necessary for the tube's operation.

E. I. D.

**Cathode ray** A cathode ray is a stream of ELECTRONS (negatively charged particles) emitted from the cathode of a gas discharge tube. The cathode ray is used in fluorescent lamps, neon tubes, kinescope or TELEVISION picture tubes, and oscilloscopes. The ray excites luminescent materials and causes them to glow. In this process, electrical energy is changed to visible radiation.

In the early 19th century, a German glassblower, Heinrich Geissler, made a glass tube which he filled with a gas at very low pressure. By sparking the tube with high voltage, he made the tube glow. When a British scientist, Sir William Crookes, experimented further by removing most of the gas, he found that the glow almost disappeared. He noticed, however, that a shadow of the center electrical terminal appeared at the end of the tube when this terminal was connected to the positive side of the high voltage and the other terminal was connected to the negative side. When the connections were reversed, *no shadow appeared*. He concluded that either invisible rays or particles were produced at the negative post and interrupted by the positive post.

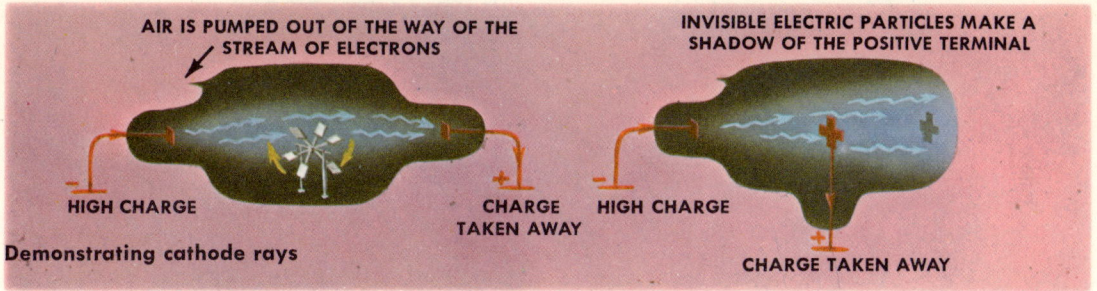

AIR IS PUMPED OUT OF THE WAY OF THE STREAM OF ELECTRONS

INVISIBLE ELECTRIC PARTICLES MAKE A SHADOW OF THE POSITIVE TERMINAL

HIGH CHARGE — CHARGE TAKEN AWAY — HIGH CHARGE — CHARGE TAKEN AWAY

Demonstrating cathode rays

In order to determine the nature of this phenomenon, he built a special low-pressure tube coated on the inside with chemicals that would glow when exposed to high voltage. Part way down the length of the tube was a round plate with a narrow slit in it so that the path of the beam could be studied. The experiment proved that the beam was bent or deflected toward the positive terminal. Since light cannot be deflected by charged plates, the theory of moving negatively charged particles emitting from the negative terminal (the CATHODE) was established. When Sir Joseph John Thomson, in the late 19th Century, wrote a summary about these negative particles of cathode rays, he called them *electrons*.               E. I. D.

**Cathode-ray tube** Cathode-ray tubes are ELECTRON beam tubes with a luminescent screen upon which the moving pattern of the beam can be seen. The cathode-ray tube may be one of two types: (1) The OSCILLOSCOPE, or oscillograph, used for graphical representation of electrical signals, and (2) the picture tube or kinescope, used for reproducing televised pictures. The physical appearance of both tubes is similar. Functionally, they differ by the number of luminous traces seen on the screen.

Three primary parts make up the tube:

1) *Envelope*—a funnel-shaped glass or metal high-vacuum enclosure which supports the electron gun and the phosphor screen. The envelope may be designed for a 1" to 22" diameter, round face; or for an 8" to 27" diagonal, rectangular face.

2) *Electron gun*—located in the slim neck of the funnel. This component produces, focuses, and deflects the electron beam. The heated CATHODE "shoots" electrons through the control grid and accelerating grid. As the focused electron beam passes the deflection grids or coils, it is rapidly moved vertically and horizontally to produce a pattern on the screen.

3) *Phosphor screen*—the wide part of the envelope which holds the phosphor-coated glass. This illuminates when struck by bombarding electrons, producing the picture or graph.               E. I. D.

SEE ALSO: CATHODE RAY, ELECTRONICS, LUMINESCENCE, TELEVISION

In the cathode ray tube the beam of electrons from the glowing filament is bent up and down, side to side, by the deflecting plates which are charged with the signal to be pictured. The electrons spray the face of the tube in the signal pattern

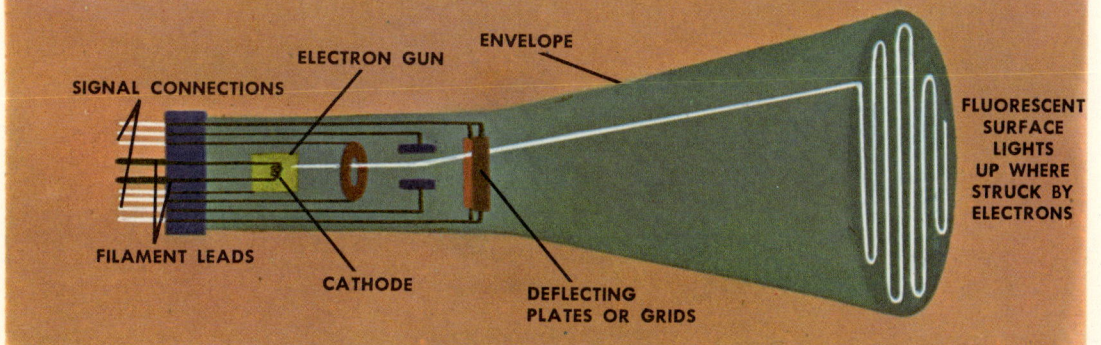

SIGNAL CONNECTIONS — ELECTRON GUN — ENVELOPE — FLUORESCENT SURFACE LIGHTS UP WHERE STRUCK BY ELECTRONS — FILAMENT LEADS — CATHODE — DEFLECTING PLATES OR GRIDS

Catnip

**Catnip** Catnip, or *catmint,* is a MINT-plant that has a strong scent. Cats like this scent. Toys made for cats often have catnip leaves inside them. Catnip leaves are a pale, gray-green color. The soft, feathery leaves are shaped like hearts.

Catnip plants grow from two to three feet tall. Many tiny flowers cluster at the tip of the long stalks. The flowers are light violet or white.

Catnip can be found growing wild in North America, although it is originally from Europe. This PERENNIAL herb is sometimes raised in old-fashioned gardens. In some places catnip leaves are used to brew a medicinal tea. M. R. L.
SEE ALSO: HERBS

**Cattail** Cattail, or *reed mace,* as it is called in England, is a wild plant which grows in marshy places. The narrow leaves will grow three to six feet tall. The strong, straight flower stem rising from the base of the leaves grows three to eight feet tall. The dark brown clump of flowers looks like the end of a cat's tail.

A cattail seed has a parachute of down. Wind may disperse the seeds great distances. Cattail leaves were only used for weaving mats and seats of chairs. The entire plant is used as a winter bouquet. J. K. K.
SEE ALSO: SEED DISPERSAL

**Cattle** see Cow, Ungulata

**Caucasoid** see Evolution of Man

Cattails
Courtesy Society For Visual Education, Inc.

Cauliflower

**Cauliflower** (KAHL-ee-flower) Cauliflower is a variety of CABBAGE. The word *cauliflower* means "stemflower." It has a solid head of white flower clusters (the part that is eaten) which grow on top of a short stalk.

Cauliflower is difficult to raise and takes special care. It will grow only in cool, moist areas. Most gardeners buy rooted cauliflower plants. When the first button-like swelling appears on the stem, the outer leaves of the plant must be tied up loosely to shade the flower. The plant should be cut when the flower buds are fully formed but not yet opened. M. R. L.

**Caustic** (KAW-stick) A caustic is a chemical substance which can burn or destroy living tissue. Caustics are alkalies (bases) used in industrial processes and in household cleaning products. The word "caustic" comes from the Greek word *kaustikos* which means "burning."

**Cave** A cave is a hollowed-out chamber in the earth. Most caves are formed deep under ground in limestone, dolomite, or other soft rock. Underground water dissolves or wears away this rock. Scientists often find the remains of early life in caves. Many people visit caves because of the beautiful sights, such as the STALAGMITES and the STALACTITES.

Mammoth Cave in Kentucky is one of the most famous caves in the United States. If a person were to explore all of Mammoth Cave's rooms and passages, he would travel about 200 miles. Some of the rooms

Inside of a cave
Courtesy Society For Visual Education, Inc.

are over fifty feet high. There are many streams and pools in Mammoth Cave. Visitors can travel in boats on some of these streams. Fish without eyes live in this water. Because the cave is dark, the fish do not need eyes for seeing. Another interesting fact about Mammoth Cave is the never changing temperature of 54° F.

Carlsbad Caverns in New Mexico are probably the largest system of caves so far discovered. Other famous caves in the United States are the Wyandotte Cave in Indiana and the Wind Cave in South Dakota.

Unlike the caves formed by underground water, *sea caves* are carved in cliffs by pounding ocean waves. Fingal's Cave on the island of Staffa, Scotland, is a famous sea cave.

Another type of cave is the *lava cave,* formed by the lava of a VOLCANO. The Singing Cave in Iceland is a lava cave.

When icebergs or glaciers melt and then freeze again, they form another kind of cave known as the *ice cave.* The Eiseisenwelt Cave in Austria is an example.

Caves have been very valuable to the scientist in his study of early man and of plant and animal life. Cave men lived in caves in southern France and northern Spain 100,000 years ago. The cave men left many paintings on the walls, showing the types of animals they hunted. By analyzing the floors of caves and ashes of fires, much of the cave man's life story has been pieced together. Many FOSSILS of early plant and animal life have been discovered in caves.                      P. F. D.

SEE ALSO: ARCHEOLOGY, GEOLOGY, GLACIER

**Caviar** (KAH-vee-are) Caviar is the roe, or eggs, of a STURGEON found in the Black or Caspian seas. The eggs, salted and canned, are considered a table delicacy by many.

**Cavity** see Tooth decay

**Cavy** see Guinea pig

**Cayenne** (kye-YENN) Cayenne is a hot-tasting ground red PEPPER. It is used in highly flavored foods such as chili and tamales. Cayenne is made from the dried, ripe fruit of several kinds of *Capsicum* plants commonly called chilies or red peppers.

There are over 200 species of the Genus *Capsicum,* all differing in size, color and taste, and all belonging to the POTATO family. They are grown in the southern zones of the world. Although their hot clear taste is strong, the aroma of the ground pepper is sweet like that of a violet. Cayenne is used also in gargles and liniments.

J. K. K.

SEE ALSO: PAPRIKA

**Cedar** (SEE-der) Cedars are evergreen trees. They belong to the PINE family. True cedars grow very slowly and become very tall. Some are over 150 feet tall. They have wide-spreading branches with leaves that look like green needles. Cones hang from the branches, and seeds are found under scales of the cones. Most people like the fresh, sweet, odor of cedar wood. This reddish-colored wood is very sturdy.

Many cedars grow in warm climates. Asia and Africa are areas where true cedars grow. The altas cedar is a native tree of North Africa. The Cedar of Lebanon that grows in Asia Minor is well-known. According to the Bible, the sturdy trunks of these cedars were used to build the huge temple buildings during the reign of King Solomon.

Native American varieties that have the characteristic cedar odor are not true cedars. The common red cedar and the white cedar are really JUNIPERS. Red cedars are used in landscaping. The wood of the white cedar is used in cedar chests because it is poisonous to insects. It is also used in making lead pencils. Poles and posts are often made of durable trunks of the red cedars of Canada, the ARBORVITAE.      M. R. L.

**Red cedar**
Courtesy Society For Visual Education, Inc.

Celery

**Celery** Celery is a vegetable which may be eaten either raw or cooked. The stalks that are eaten are the basal parts of the leaves, the petroles. The "heart" is the short stem. Celery came from a wild, bitter HERB used centuries ago in medicines.

Celery, a member of the PARSLEY family, is raised in moist soil in California, Florida, Michigan, New York, and Colorado. It is blanched by using boards or special blanching paper to shut out the sun from the fleshy stalks.                           J. K. K.

**Celestial navigation** Before RADIO and RADAR were developed, sailors had to guide their ships by the sun and the stars when they were out of sight of familiar landmarks. Finding one's way by the heavenly bodies is called *celestial navigation*.

Celestial navigators use the sun, the moon, four planets and 30 or 40 stars. They need to know the earthly positions of these heavenly bodies, that is, where they would land if they suddenly dropped straight down to earth. Because the earth moves, these bodies change their positions constantly. The navigator needs to know their positions for every minute, even second, of every day and night.

The *Nautical Almanac* gives all of these changing positions based on Greenwich time. The navigator sets his very fine watch, the chronometer, for Greenwich time. With a sextant he measures the altitude of a star and its angle above the horizon. Then he can determine how far he is from the earthly position of the star. He knows that he is somewhere on a circle of a known radius and a known center. He observes two or more heavenly bodies, makes his calculations, and draws the circles of his position on a map. Where these circles cross is the position of his ship.     C. L. K.
SEE ALSO: NAVIGATION

**Cellophane** Cellophane is a material made from CELLULOSE, the chemical substance which lines the walls of plant cells. It is a tough, moisture-proof, gas-proof material, manufactured in various thicknesses and colors. A common use of cellophane is for packaging foods.

The first quantity production of cellophane occurred in 1911 when J. E. Brandenburger designed a machine which made a continuous roll of the strong, transparent film. He named this product cellophane, a combination of the words *cellulose* and *diaphane* (transparency).

Additional uses of cellophane are for wrapping munitions to protect them from the weather, for preserving print, for sealing or mending materials, and for winding electric wire.               V. B. I.

A sextant tells the altitude of a star. The altitude is the angle between two lines—one, from ship to star and, two, from ship to point on Earth directly below star. The exact position of the ship is calculated from readings from several stars

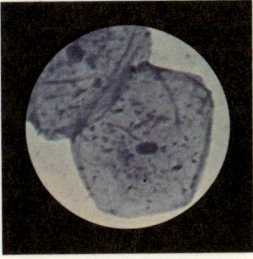

Cells from inside the cheek are thin, flat and arranged for smoothness and flexibility. (900 times magnification)

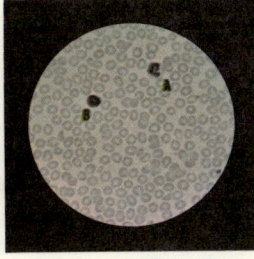

Red blood cells have no nuclei and do not reproduce themselves. A and B are white cells with nuclei. (500x)

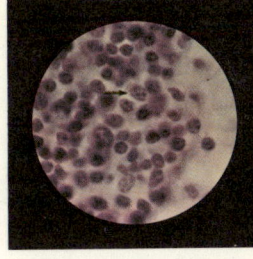

Lymph cells (arrow) fight disease like white blood cells. Surrounding cells are of lymph gland. (1200x)

Bone cells (at A) make hardening chemicals. A blood vessel (B) and canals are also shown. (300x)

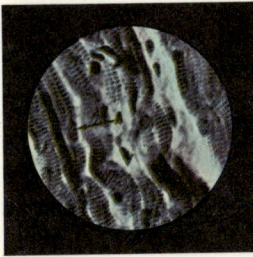

Voluntary muscle cells look like striped ribbons. Long fibers within the cell contract. Nucleus is at A. (900x)

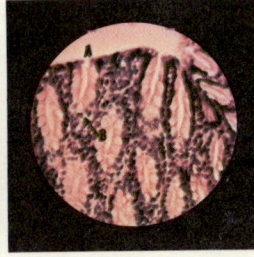

Gland cells in large intestine secrete digestive substances. A is a gland with duct. B is nucleus of the cell. (360x)

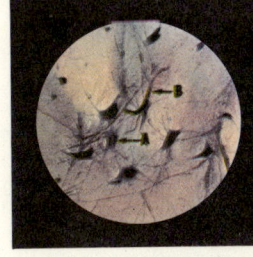

Nerve cells from the spinal cord. A is the cell body from which branches spread out. B is a blood vessel. (60x)

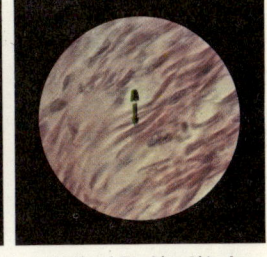

Involuntary muscles are not striped and are shorter than voluntary. A points to a good example. (900x)

Photo-micrographs by National Teaching Aids, Inc.

**Cells** If a school building had only one big classroom, all of the boys and girls would have to work together. While some were trying to study, others would be listening to music or playing basketball. Schools have to be divided into separate rooms, so that people can do different things in different rooms.

Scientists used to think that the smallest part of a tree was its smallest leaf or root. When the microscope was invented, they discovered that all plants and animals, like school buildings, are really made up of tiny rooms, called *cells*. Each cell is surrounded by a thin skin or membrane, just as rooms are surrounded by walls.

Schools are built of many materials, such as brick, wood or steel. Plants and animals are built of one material, called *protoplasm*. This is the only living material known. Just as boys and girls are always moving from one room to the next, materials in protoplasm move from one cell to another. While students pass through doors, protoplasm moves through tiny openings in the membrane.

When plants and animals, like the blue-green ALGAE or the AMEBA, consist of one cell, that cell must do all of the work. When organisms are built of many cells, these cells are able to divide the work. All cells have personal housekeeping duties, such as taking in food and getting rid of waste products. Just as many doctors are specialists in blood disease or bone surgery, most cells are specialists in certain parts of the body. These specialized cells work in teams. Together, they form a *tissue*. The heart and the brain are examples of organs made up of many tissues.

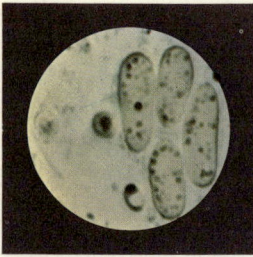

Bacteria are one-celled plants. Unlike most cells, bacteria have no nuclei. (1500x)

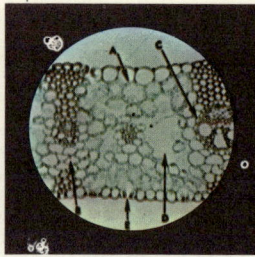

Parts of a leaf: A—clear cell; B—nucleus; C—vein; D—air space; E—breathing pore. (300x)

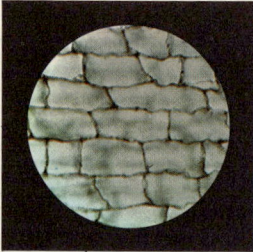

Photo-micrographs by National Teaching Aids, Inc.

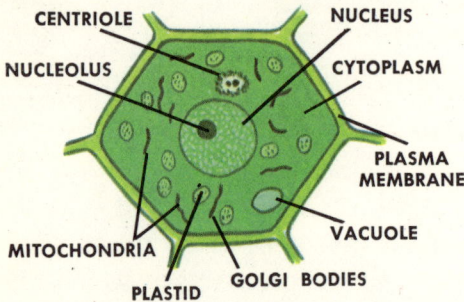

Dead cork cells have no inner material. Hooke discovered cells from cork. (300x)

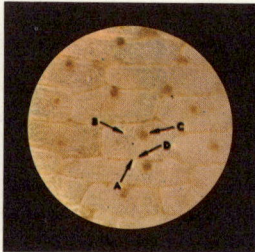

Stained onion skin shows A—cell wall, B—cytoplasm, C—nucleus, D—membrane. (200x)

A diagrammatic generalized cell

Protoplasm is a mixture of chemicals. Carbon, hydrogen, oxygen, and nitrogen are the main elements in protoplasm. Molecules of these are put together to form ORGANIC COMPOUNDS—carbohydrates, fats, and proteins, as well as inorganic compounds—water and minerals. Since the molecules are constantly reacting with one another, protoplasm is always in a chemical turmoil. The molecules around the outside of the cell form a skin called the *plasma membrane.* Tiny pores in the membrane are gateways through which molecules may pass. However, the membrane is very selective. It accepts or rejects molecules as they are needed by the cell.

The cell consists of a *nucleus,* which is surrounded by *cytoplasm* (cell plasm). The nucleus is like the teacher in the classroom, since it is responsible for the main activities of the cell. It is a large jelly-like mass usually surrounded by ·another membrane. It is a house for the CHROMOSOMES, the carriers of GENES. The nucleus also has its own small nucleus called the *nucleolus.*

Within the cytoplasm, many small granules, rods, and droplets are suspended. Although these have been given various names, scientists are not positive of their individual functions. Rounded bodies, called *mitochondria,* are probably responsible for the exchange of gases in the cell. Tiny granules, called *microsomes,* are probably the chief centers for the putting together of proteins. *Golgi bodies,* which look like fine mesh, are probably responsible for the manufacture of secretion products, since many are found in cells of glands. Oval bodies, called PLASTIDS, are found in plant cells. These may contain pigment or coloring matter. When they are green, they contain CHLOROPHYLL and are centers for PHOTOSYNTHESIS. A tiny body, called a *centriole,* is located just outside the nucleus. Occurring in animal cells and in some plant cells, it functions during cell reproduction.

Cytoplasm also contains much unabsorbed food which is found either in granules or *vacuoles.* Vacuoles are small spaces filled with solids, liquids, or gases and surrounded by a membrane. They may be filled with raw food or waste material. They may be centers for storage of starch, fat, or water.

Certain types of cells may have an extra wall surrounding the plasma membrane. Since plants need protection and support against gravity, plant cells have rigid, CELLULOSE walls. While animal cells do not have true cell walls, often the outer layer of cells secretes a thick covering such as the CHITIN, found in arthropods.

Cells produce new cells by dividing. Since new cells can arise only from existing cells, all life is continuous. All living cells of today have come from ancestor cells which existed billions of years ago.   E. P. L. SEE ALSO: MITOSIS AND MEIOSIS, NERVE CELL, PLANT TISSUE, PROTOZOA

**Cells, in series and parallel** see Battery, Electricity

**Celluloid** Celluloid is an artificial material used as a substitute for bone, ivory and hard rubber. It is hard, transparent, elastic and very flammable. It is made from nitrates of CELLULOSE.

**Cellulose** (SELL-yuh-lohs) Cellulose helps the stem of a flower stand up straight and hold the blossom towards the sun.

All green plants manufacture cellulose. It is the chemical substance which makes up the walls of PLANT cells. Over 30% of a plant is cellulose.

Cellulose is a CARBOHYDRATE that many animals use for food. Man cannot digest it but needs it as roughage in his diet. The leaves and stalks of celery and spinach hold large quantities of cellulose.

Cloth is made from the cellulose in the fibers of a cotton plant. Products made of wood are partly cellulose. PAPER is almost completely composed of cellulose.　　P. G. B.

Concrete mixer

**Cement** Cement is a soft gray powder that is made from lime, silica and alumina. It is mixed with water and sand to make mortar. This material will hold bricks together in buildings. Concrete is a mixture of cement, sand, gravel and water, and it is used in making pavements and sidewalks. It is also very useful in building dams, bridges, and canal locks.

About two-thirds of the material used in making cement is lime which comes from limestone and various shells. These rock-like substances are crushed and ground up in huge machines. This material is then dried and ground again before it goes to the kiln for roasting. This process gives it its binding properties. The final step is the addition of a small amount of GYPSUM and a final grinding to powder.　　D. E. Z.

**Cenozoic Era** (see-nuh-ZO-ick) Cenozoic Era is the present period in the earth's history. It is also called the Age of Mammals and the Age of Man. During the 60 million years of this era, present-day animals and plants came into being. Once mountain ranges and lakes were formed, the climate grew cooler until ice covered part of the earth.

### TERTIARY PERIOD

The era is divided into two periods and six epochs, listed from oldest to youngest. The *Tertiary* period extended from 60 million to one million years ago. The ocean covered the southeastern United States. The Sierra Nevadas in the United States, the Alps in Europe, and the Himalayas in Asia were formed. There were many volcanoes.

FOSSILS of the major plant groups are found in the Tertiary rock layers. As the climate grew cooler and drier, grasses replaced the forests. Only those plants that shed leaves to live through the cold survived in the northern regions.

One-celled, coin-shaped protozoans (nummulites) were abundant in the seas. Their shells helped make thick limestone formations. Mammals lived all over the world. Bones and teeth found in the sediment layers show the changes in animal forms for each successive epoch. Most of the world's oil and many metals are found in these rock layers.

The *Paleocene* epoch is the oldest division of the Tertiary period. The climate was wet and semi-tropical. The paleocene rocks were sandstone, shale and low grade coal. The mammals were small and unspecialized.

The *Eocene* was an epoch of expanding seas and large lakes. South America was separate from North America. New animals appeared. There were blunt-toothed, dull-witted mammals (creodonts), the first horses (Eohippus) and small ancestors of the deer, pig and camel. Rabbits, moles, insects, monkeys, bats and whales existed at this time. Eocene is often classed with Paleocene as one epoch.

The *Oligocene,* middle Tertiary epoch, was marked by volcanoes and floods. Fossils found in the sand and silt of the White River beds indicate that the animals in North America forty million years ago resembled

**Huge glaciers covered much of North America during the Pleistocene epoch of the Cenozoic Era. They left the terrain much as it is today**

those of central Africa today.

The *Miocene* epoch, the high point of mammal life, developed the MASTODON, panther, bear, weasel, skunk, sloth and the armadillo. The Alps and Himalaya mountains were formed. There were probably land links between Asia and North America, and between Africa and Europe. Florida emerged.

The *Pliocene,* or last Tertiary epoch, was drier and cooler. The mammals of the warm climates were extinct or lived near the Equator.

### QUATERNARY PERIOD

The Quaternary period is the most recent time span of less than a million years.

The *Pleistocene* epoch is the ice age and the age of man. Huge glaciers, thousands of feet thick, like those of Antarctica and Greenland covered Northern Europe and North America as far south as the Ohio River. Dried and frozen skeletons of great mammals have been found: MAMMOTHS, beavers as large as bears, and wolves as tall

as man. It is certain that man developed during this time.

Sediments and fossils indicate that extensive glaciers were followed by warmer climates when the ice sheet slowly melted, leaving fresh water lakes. Winds blew fine rock over the great plains forming its fertile soil. Sand piled up in dunes.

Four glacial and three interglacial stages have been charted. Cores of sediment brought up from the ocean beds indicate there may have been from five to fifteen cold-warm cycles. Time estimates for the ice age vary from 280,000 years to 800,000 years.

The last ice sheet melted from the United States about 11,000 years ago. The present ice-free years were called a new or *Recent* epoch. However, many geologists now think that this is still the Ice Age and that glaciers might begin to form again, perhaps in ten to fifty thousand years.          A. P. M.

SEE ALSO: EVOLUTION OF MAN, GEOLOGIC TIME TABLE, GLACIAL AGES, PALEONTOLOGY

**Centaurus** (senn-TAW-rus) Centaurus, or the Centaur, is a CONSTELLATION that can be seen from the southern part of the earth. It is famous because its brightest star, *Alpha Centauri,* is the closest star to the earth visible to the eye.

Alpha Centauri is one of the twenty brightest stars. It is only about four light years away from the earth, or about 25 trillion miles. Another one of Centaurus's stars, *Proxima Centauri,* is even closer to the earth than Alpha Centauri. Proxima Centauri is a very faint star, a dwarf, and can be seen only with the help of a telescope.

*Beta Centauri,* Centaurus's second brightest star, is also one of the twenty brightest stars. Alpha and Beta Centauri are sometimes called the *Southern Pointers* because they point to another famous southern hemisphere constellation, the Southern Cross. Alpha Centauri is a beautiful yellow star. Beta Centauri is blue-white.

The stars and constellations of the southern hemisphere were first noticed and named during the Middle Ages, when adventurers began to explore the southern and western world.

In July and August, people in southern Florida and Texas can sometimes see Centaurus. In the early evening during those months it would be very low on the horizon in the extreme south of the United States.

                                    C. L. K.

SEE ALSO: ALPHA, CRUX

**Centaurus, the Centaur**

**Centigrade** The centigrade or *Celsius* scale is a temperature measurement index. In this system the ice point and the steam point of water, under standard atmospheric pressure, differ by a 100 degree interval. This scale is used in Europe and in most all scientific work, although the American household uses the FAHRENHEIT scale.

In 1949, the Bureau of Standards and other national laboratories in the United States recommended that scientists and industrial workers uphold the 1948 adoption of the Conference of Weights and Measures and change the degree designation from centigrade to Celsius, in honor of the man who promoted this scale.     D. L. D.

SEE ALSO: TEMPERATURE SCALES

**Centipede**

**Centipede** The centipede gets its name because of its many legs. Centipedes are the "wolves" of the *myriapoda* group. They hunt small animals that live on or in the soil. They kill their prey by poison excreted from the first pair of legs, called the *poison claws.*

Each body segment of the centipede has a single pair of legs. When the insects are freshly hatched, they have six or seven pairs of legs. However, as adults they have over fifteen pairs of legs. Certain centipedes which live deep in the soil have nearly two hundred pairs of legs. The name *centipede* means "100 feet."

There is a house centipede, found in such places as the damp walls of basements, which differs in appearance from its relatives. It has fifteen very long legs, which drop off when touched. These centipedes assist man by feeding on insect pests of the household.     V. V. N.

SEE ALSO: ARTHROPODA, MILLIPEDE

## WHAT IS CENTRIFUGAL FORCE?

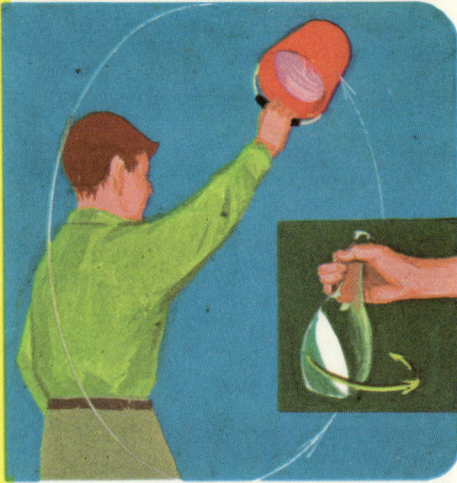

1  Fill a pail one-third full of water. Swing it quickly up over your head and down in a circular fashion. The water clings to the bottom of the pail and does not spill out.
2  Put an inch of water in a round vase. Turn it rapidly sidewise. The water will leave the bottom and cling to the round sides.
3  Centrifugal force keeps an object moving in a circle the farthest away from the center of revolution.

**Centrifugal and centripetal forces** If a ball is whirled at the end of a string in a circular motion, it would seem as if the ball were suddenly very heavy and were pulling harder as it is whirled faster. The force of the string pulling the ball toward the center of the circle is the *centripetal force*. The force seeming to act on the string by the ball is the *centrifugal force*.

An apparent outward force on an object rotating about an axis is met with an equal inward force in order to continue the rotation. The outward force is centrifugal and the inward force is centripetal. This phenomenon is an example of Sir Isaac Newton's third law of motion: "Every force is accompanied by an equal and opposite reacting force."

The reaction of the centripetal force is the result of the ball's tending to continue on a path tangent to the circle. The string keeps pulling the ball in, to keep it in a circular

✳ **THINGS TO DO**

## CAN ONE INCREASE CENTRIFUGAL FORCE?

1  Fasten a one pound weight to the end of a strong string. Holding the other end of the string, start swinging the weight in a circle. Swing it as fast as possible. Feel the pull on the arm.
2  Replace the small weight with a heavier one. Repeat the circular motion. Is the pull on the arm greater?
3  Centrifugal force is the pull of an object which is moving in a circle. Increasing the weight and speed of the moving object will increase the centrifugal force. Centripetal force is exerted by the arm to keep the object from flying out. This is the equal and opposite of centrifugal force.

motion, instead of allowing it to go straight —on the tangent. When the string is released, the ball does not fly straight out as centrifugal force would indicate, nor does the ball pull in toward the center as centripetal force suggests. Releasing the string eliminates the centripetal force since there is no force pulling the ball inward. At the same time, the equal and opposite reaction, centrifugal force, which is actually the pull of the string on the center axis, also disappears.

The CENTRIFUGE is a device which uses the principle of centrifugal force for separating liquids or liquids and solids into the individual components. The separation of cream from milk, and water from laundry illustrates this. Engines are sometimes equipped with centrifugal governors to control their speed. As rotating weights move outward, the attached linkage changes the setting of the engine's throttle.     E. I. D.

SEE ALSO: NEWTON, SIR ISAAC

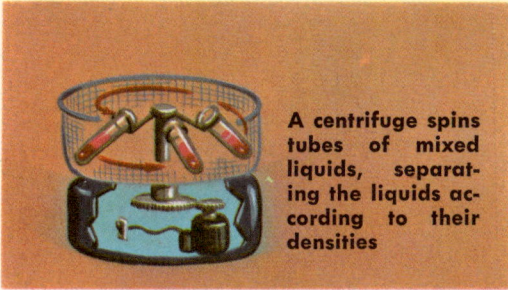

A centrifuge spins tubes of mixed liquids, separating the liquids according to their densities

From ground-hugging leaves, the famous century plant sends blossoms high in the air
Courtesy Society For
Visual Education, Inc.

**Centrifuge** (SENN-truh-fewj) A centrifuge is a rotating machine having a hollow rotor. A mixture of liquids, or solids and liquids may be fed into it and then subjected to high speeds and centrifugal force, so that the mixture will be separated into its component parts (because of the difference in densities of the components). Cream separators, centrifugal oil purifiers, sugar centrifugals, and centrifugal laundry dryers are examples of such machines.

High-speed centrifuges of the cream separator type have over four hundred different applications in the chemical, petroleum, and food industries. Small centrifuges capable of extremely high speeds are used in research. D. L. D.

**Centriole** see Cell

**Centripetal** see Centrifugal and centripetal forces

**Century plant** The century plant is a desert plant with large, thick leaves which store food and water. Many people have the mistaken idea that century plants bloom only every 100 years, once every century. Different kinds of century plants flower at different times, but none of them waits 100 years to bloom. The flowers grow in clusters on the upper part of a tall stalk.

In Mexico, fermented sap from the century plant is used to make an intoxicating beverage called *pulque*.

The century plant belongs to the *Amaryllidaceae* family. It is also commonly called *Agave*. J. D. B.

**Cepheus** (SEE-fyoos) Cepheus is a group of stars that looks like a triangle on top of a square. It is not a very bright CONSTELLATION, but in the northern part of the world it can be seen on almost any clear night. It is near POLARIS, the bright star in the Dipper.

Cepheus was the name of an ancient king of Ethiopia. Cepheus; his wife, CASSIOPEIA; their daughter, Andromeda; and Perseus are a group of constellations known as the Royal Family. The Greeks believed that Cepheus was one of the men called Argonauts who went with Jason to find the Golden Fleece. In another legend, Cepheus had to offer his daughter Andromeda as a sacrifice to a sea monster because Cassiopeia had boasted that she was more beautiful than the sea nymphs. Perseus rescued Andromeda.

Some of the stars in the Cepheus constellation are "variable" stars, which means that their brightness varies. Delta, the fourth brightest star of the group, is especially variable. Stars of this type are called "Cepheid variables." There is a rhythmical pattern of change in brightness which astronomers can study and determine the true brightness of the star. C. L. K.

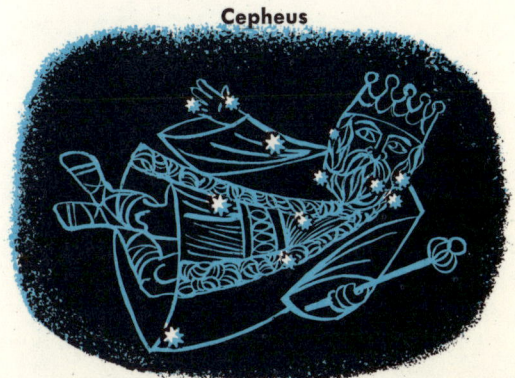

Cepheus

**Wheat    Corn    Rice    Oats    Barley**

**Cereal grains** Cereal grains are GRASSES. Seeds from these grasses can be ground into meal or flour. Flour is used to make bread and other starchy foods. Sometimes the whole seed is eaten. Animals raised for meat and dairy products are fed cereal grains. The common cereal grains are WHEAT, CORN, RICE, OATS, and BARLEY.

The best grasslands are often called "breadbaskets," because they grow grain so well. Today, the world's most important "breadbaskets" are in the prairies of the United States and Canada, the pampas of Argentina, the grain belts of Australia and the Russian Ukraine. These areas produce most of the grains on the world market except rice. Most rice is produced in Asia and near-by islands. Rice provides the main food for about half the human race.

All the grains today were first grown by the Stone Age man. They have been improved, but modern man has not developed one new cereal grain.       M. R. L.

**Cerebellum** (sehr-uh-BELL-uhm) The cerebellum is sometimes called the *hinder* or *little* brain. It is located at the back of the skull beneath the CEREBRUM, the first or largest part of the brain. The cerebellum controls the power of balancing and helps the muscles work together. If it is injured, a person may not be able to stand straight or walk in a straight line. The cerebellum has control over the sense of position so that one knows whether his legs are crossed at the knee or ankle without looking at them. The

**The cerebellum is located beneath and behind the main part of the brain**

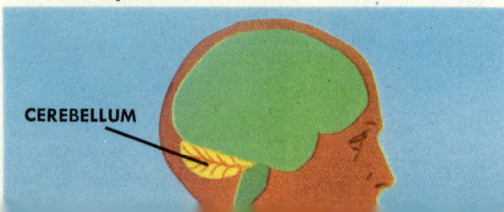

CEREBELLUM

cerebellum is highly developed in birds because the birds must sense their exact position and maintain perfect balance.

The cerebellum is the coordinator of the BRAIN. If the muscles did not work together and in order, there would be confusion. Tremor, staggering gaits, and defective ability to use alternating muscle groups may result if the cerebellum is damaged.

The cerebellum is composed of a superficial layer of gray matter and a central mass of white connecting fibers. Sometimes this core of white fibers is referred to as the "tree of life" because it has a branch-like appearance. The cerebellum has two hemispheres that are connected by transverse fibers.       M. I. L.

**Cerebral palsy** (SER-uh-bruhl PALL-zee) Cerebral palsy is a disease of the body which starts at birth or even before birth. About one or two babies out of every 1000 are affected. The usual cause is a defect in the development of the BRAIN of the baby, or a breaking down of the brain cells while being formed. Occasionally some injury at birth causes the condition.

When the brain of these individuals is examined it is found to be small and shrunken. The tissue is extremely hard. The membranes covering the brain can be thickened, hard and adherent to the underlying tissue. Many times the infant may be small with delicate physical development. In mild cases the condition is not noted until it is found that the baby does not walk or talk at the expected time. In the second or third year of the child's life, more signs of the disease become apparent. The legs are usually the most severely affected and this results in a weakness which makes walking difficult.

Treatment of this condition requires very special attention. Although these children may seem retarded in their mental accomplishments many of them are brighter than they appear. The slowness is often due to their physical handicap in getting about. Special care and special courses of study can be of great benefit.       H. K. S.

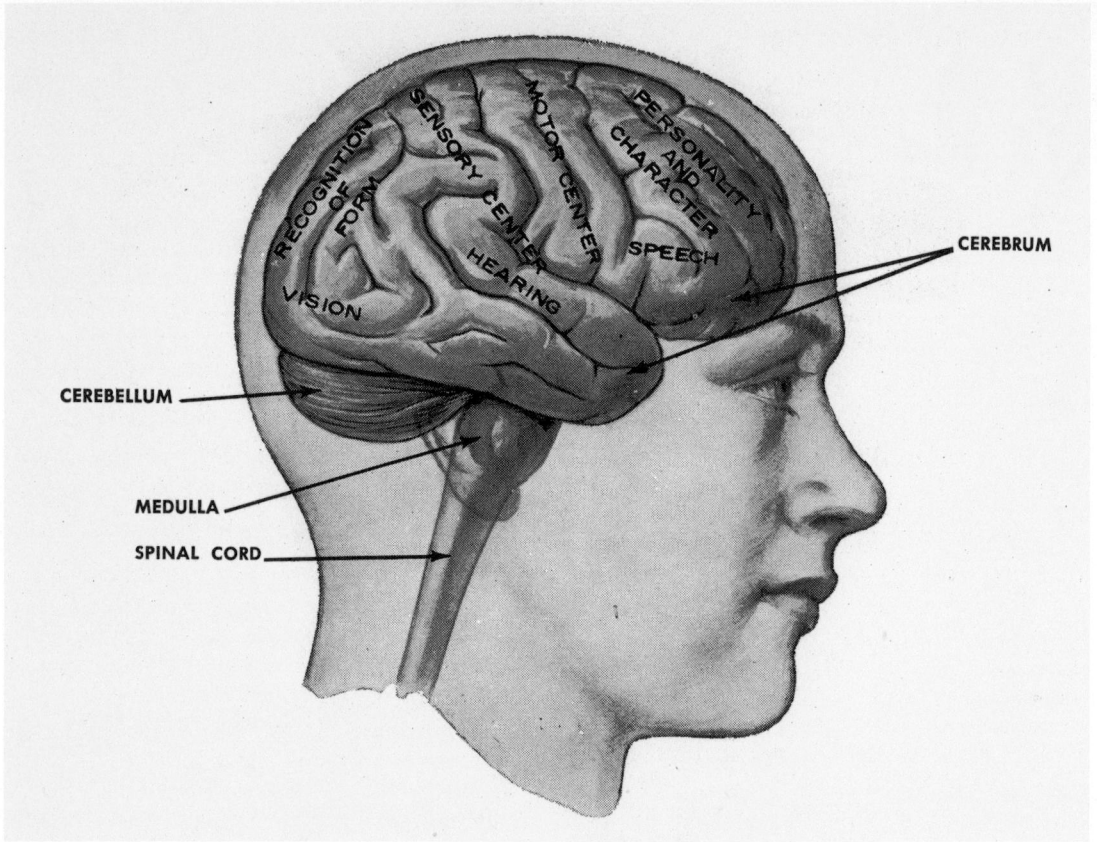

Labels on illustration: RECOGNITION OF FORM, SENSORY CENTER, MOTOR CENTER, PERSONALITY AND CHARACTER, SPEECH, HEARING, VISION, CEREBRUM, CEREBELLUM, MEDULLA, SPINAL CORD

TODAY'S HEALTH, published by AMERICAN MEDICAL ASSOCIATION

**Cerebrum** (Ser-REE-brum) The cerebrum is the largest or main part of the BRAIN. The cerebrum controls the ability to think. Man is probably the only animal that has this ability. Each part of the cerebrum has a duty to perform. One part controls imagination and memory. Other parts control the senses of smell, taste, touch, hearing, sight and speech. One area controls purposeful movement of the muscles. This makes it possible for a person to throw a ball, dance, or jump rope at a selected time.

The cerebrum is like a switchboard. The switchboard receives the dial tones, and soon telephones in far away places ring. The cerebrum receives the impulses and directs the body into action. The impulses travelling the nerve cells are the messengers to and from the cerebrum.

The cerebrum has many ridges and indentations. Each person has a cerebrum of a different design just as each person has

a different fingerprint or handwriting. If the cerebrum is injured in one area the functions or the sense that the injured area controls may be impaired.

The cerebrum is composed of gray and white matter. The gray matter is on the surface in what is called the *cortex*. The gray matter consists of large masses of nerve cells. The nerve cells are interlaced and connected in endless ways. The cerebrum is partially divided into right and left hemispheres by a cleft, the longitudinal fissure. Each hemisphere has four lobes, the frontal, parietal, occipital and temporal. The *frontal* lobe controls muscular activity. The *parietal* lobe is the center for pressure, pain and temperature responses. The *occipital* is concerned with sight, and the *temporal* area receives impulses from the tongue, nose, and ears. There are nerves that connect each lobe with every other part of the brain. There are many combinations of nerve fibers. Fibers from one hemisphere cross to the opposite side at various levels. If the right side of the cerebrum is injured, the left side may be affected.     M. I. L.

SEE ALSO: NERVOUS SYSTEM

**Greenland whale**

**Dolphin**

**Cereus, night-blooming** see Night-blooming plants

**Cerium** (SEER-ee-uhm) Cerium is the most abundant metal of the group of metals known as the RARE EARTHS. It is iron-gray in color. It has a hardness similar to that of tin and silver.

Jons Berzelius and Wilhelm Hisinger discovered this ELEMENT in 1803. Another scientist, Martin Klaproth, working independently, also discovered cerium. Berzelius named it after the asteroid Ceres.

Its atomic number is 58, and its atomic weight is 140.13.

Cerium is used in the iron industry to make alloys. Cerium is also used in the manufacture of VACUUM TUBES and porcelain coatings for signs.     V. B. I.

**Cesium** (SEE-zee-uhm) Cesium is a soft, silvery-white metal, a member of the RARE EARTH group of ELEMENTS. It tarnishes instantly in air and must be kept under kerosene. It is similar to SODIUM in that it reacts with water.

Gustav Kirchhoff and Robert Bunsen discovered cesium in 1860. It is found mainly in the mineral monazite in India, Brazil and Idaho.

The main uses of the element are in the manufacture of radio and power tubes and in the treatment of shock.

Cesium has an atomic number of 55 and an atomic weight of 132.91.     V. B. I.

**Cetacea** (sih-TAY-shuh) Cetacea is the order of mammals that includes WHALES and PORPOISES. Like all mammals, they are warm blooded, breathe air, and have skin. Cetaceans differ from most mammals because they live only in the water, have no hind limbs, and have no connection between the nose and mouth.

All have paddle-like *flippers* for forelimbs and swim by using their *flukes* (horizontally flattened tails). They also have a layer of fat called *blubber* just under their skin and have a nose opening, *blowhole,* on top of their heads.

Cetaceans live in salt water, and many migrate great distances. They are seldom found in tropical waters although they go to warm water to bear young.

The three groups of Cetacea are the *whalebone whales* (such as the Greenland whale), the *toothed whales* (such as the dolphin and sperm whales, and the *fossil whales.*

A few of the aquatic adaptations of cetaceans are: (1) blubber which serves as stored food, as a heat insulator, and as a protection against increased water pressure at great depths; (2) more blood for their size than any other mammal; (3) ribs flexibly attached to the sternum for great chest expansion; (4) no upper vertebral processes for vertical tail flexibility. J. K. L.

**Chain reaction** A chain reaction is a series of molecular or atomic changes of a substance, in which, once the series is started, each change causes (sets off) the next one. The products of the first change affect the now-altered substance and cause a second change in which energy or other products are again released, and they in turn cause a third change in the constitution of the substance. This reaction may go on until some desired goal is reached.

SEE: NUCLEAR SCIENCE, NUCLEAR SCIENCE GLOSSARY

**Chalcedony** see Quartz

CHALK (WHITE) LIMESTONE

Chalk magnified to show types of crustaceans that form this soft, porous limestone
Courtesy Society For Visual Education, Inc.

**Chalk** Chalk is a soft, porous, white or grayish-white limestone made up of minute, marine shells. It was formed as mud on the bottom of an ancient sea and differs from pure limestone because it was not hardened as much. It is still soft and can be rubbed off.

Chalk deposits are found on the White Cliffs of Dover, England, in France, and in Western Kansas. They contain preserved skeletons of extinct sea serpents, flying reptiles, birds and fishes.

Chalk is made into whiting for manufacturing of rubber goods, paint, putty, soft polishing powders, tooth powder, Portland cement and top dressing for soils. Chalk for writing on blackboards is made of MAGNESIA.                                J. K. K.

SEE ALSO: CALCIUM CARBONATE

**Chameleon** (kuh-MEE-lee-un) Chameleons are a group of tree LIZARDS. They are about six inches long and have bulging eyes, long curling tails, and feet which grasp like hands. Chameleons are well-known for their ability to quickly change the color of their bodies.

Insects are the favorite food of this slow-moving lizard. It catches them with its long sticky tongue and chews them with its sharp little teeth.

The bulging eyes of the chameleon work independently of each other. While one eye is looking up, the other can look down. The chameleon is found mainly in South Asia, Africa, and Madagascar.

The chameleon is not the only kind of lizard that can change the color of its body. Scientists have found that this ability is controlled by changes in temperature, light and other reactions to environment.

The American lizard, which many girls and boys keep as a pet, is often called a chameleon, but it is not a true member of the chameleon family. This little lizard should be kept in a warm, sunny place and should be fed flies, mealworms, and drops of water.                                D. J. A.

SEE ALSO: REPTILIA

**Changes of state** see Physical states and changes; Substances, properties of

**Channel** A channel is any natural or man-made bed in which a stream of water runs. Many people confuse channel with CANAL. A canal is a channel which is man-made for navigation or for irrigating land. A channel may also be known as the deeper part of a river, harbor or strait.

Schiaparelli, the Italian astronomer, found "canali" on MARS in 1877. After he published his findings in Italian, English-speaking astronomers, anxious to criticize or praise Schiaparelli, used the word "canal" to imply they were man-made. There is disagreement among astronomers today whether there are canals or channels on the planet Mars.                                J. K. K.

True chameleon

Courtesy Society For Visual Education, Inc.

American lizard

✳ **THINGS TO DO**

## HOW TO MAKE CHARCOAL

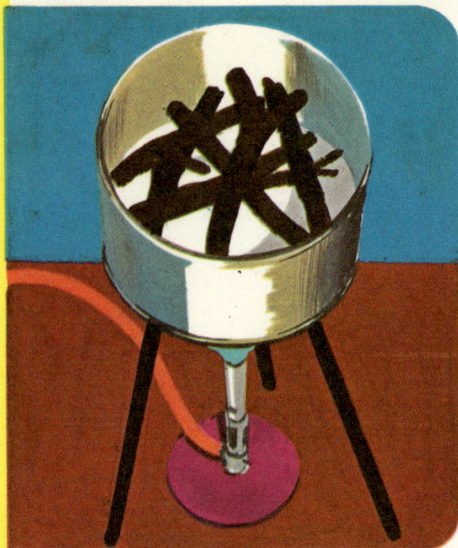

**Materials: coffee can, hardwood, bunsen burner or stove**

1   This should be done only when an older person is helping.

2   Puncture a hole in the lid of a coffee can. Place several small sticks of hardwood in the can. Replace the lid.

3   Heat the can over a bunsen burner or other heat source to drive out the water vapor in the wood.

4   As wood gas escapes from the hole light a match to it until the gas is all burned up. Remove the can from the heat and allow to cool.

5   The sticks of wood are now charcoal.

**Charcoal** Charcoal is a black, porous substance, mostly pure CARBON. It comes from animal or vegetable matter that has not been completely burned. A burned match is charcoal.

*Bone black,* a charcoal obtained from bones of animals, is used in refining sugar. LAMPBLACK, a charcoal made from oil, is used in making paints and inks. Charcoal, which is used for fuel, is made from hardwood. It is also used to broil meats and as an ingredient in black gunpowder.

Because it is porous, charcoal is used to absorb odors. Charcoal can be placed in a refrigerator to remove odors.    J. K. K.

**Chard** see Swiss chard

**Charge** see Battery, Electricity

**Charged particles** Charged particles are the tiny building blocks of atoms. They appear whenever atoms are disturbed. Stars constantly shoot charged particles through space. Streams of charged particles are called *rays,* or RADIATION.

These atomic parts are identified by their position in the atom, and by their size, weight, and behavior. Behavior partly depends on how these are charged. Some particles electrically attract each other; others repel. Of two attracting particles, one is positive and the other is negative. Particles of the same charge repel one another. Particles with no electrical attraction are called neutral.

The basic particles of an atom are *electrons* (negatively charged), *protons* (positively charged), and *neutrons* (neutral, or no charge).

There are other particles whose size and changeability make identification difficult. These subatomic particles include positrons, antiprotons, mesons, and neutrinos.

Still others, actual nuclei of certain atoms, also are called particles. One is the alpha particle (helium nucleus). Others are deutrons and tritons. Scientists are discovering more.

Machines called ACCELERATORS, or "atom smashers," isolate and use charged particles. They direct and accelerate the particles to bombard nuclei. Both alpha particles and protons are used.    D. J. I.
SEE ALSO: ATOM, NUCLEAR ENERGY

**Charioteer** see Auriga

**Charles' Law** Charles' Law is a statement concerning the action of a GAS or vapor in relation to its temperature, volume and pressure.

The *kinetic theory* of gases assumes that all gases are made up of tiny particles called MOLECULES. These molecules are very small compared to the distance which separates one particle from another. Since these molecules are in a constant state of motion, they bump into, or collide, with one another and also with the walls of the container which holds a gas. Because they are constantly moving about, each molecule has a certain amount of energy and this amount is about the same for each.

If the temperature of the gas is increased, the energy of each of the particles is also increased and they begin to move faster. If the volume of the container remains the same, the increased speed of their movement causes them to collide with the walls of the container more often and the pressure is increased. However, if the pressure is to remain the same as before, the volume containing the gas must be increased as the temperature is increased.

Hence, Charles' Law states: the volume of a gas at a constant pressure varies directly with the absolute temperature.     A. E. L.

**Chat** Chat is a name given to several species of birds of the WARBLER family. The yellow-breasted chat and long-tailed chat are found in the United States.

Arthur A. Allen

**Yellow-breasted chat**

**Cheese** see Dairy products

**Cheetah** see Cat family

**Chemical change** Chemical change is a re-arranging of ATOMS to form different kinds of materials. Energy of some sort such as heat usually is present when these changes come about. There are examples of chemical change in iron becoming rust, in burning fuels changing to smoke and ashes, and in dry cells producing ELECTRICITY. Chemical changes are constantly going on around and in man. They enable the body to use oxygen breathed and the food eaten. Plants make food through chemical change. Life would not continue without these important processes.

## ✳ THINGS TO DO

### MAKING NEW MATERIALS FROM OLD

A chemical change occurs when materials are combined to make a product which has entirely different properties than the original materials.

1  Heat a slice of bread in a toaster or oven until it is black. It has changed to charcoal.

2  Mix two tablespoons of vinegar in a cup of milk. It forms curds.

3  Rub egg over a silver spoon. After an hour it will become tarnished.

or

Cover a silver coin with sulfur till the coin is black. Sulfur and silver combine to form silver sulfide.

4  Put iron filings in a jar. Sprinkle them with water. In the presence of moisture iron combines with oxygen to form rust.

5  Heat sugar until it is brown and turns to carmel.

6  Combine water, iron sulfate, and tannic acid to make ink.

In chemical change, the *electron* arrangement of the atom or molecule is altered, *not the nucleus* as in nuclear reactions. During chemical change, electrons in the atoms are borrowed, lent or shared. The atoms which lend or borrow electrons become known as IONS. The atoms as ions are chemically active—some more so than others.

Some changes in appearance are merely physical changes. Physical change usually accompanies chemical change, while chemical change doesn't necessarily accompany physical change. For example, if a rock is ground into dust, the physical appearance is changed but not the chemical nature of the atoms of the rock. The dust is merely fine pieces of rock; likewise, when sawing a board in two, one has simply sliced between atoms and not through them. On the other hand, when a match is lit, the match disappears and new products result. Here are both chemical and physical changes. A material changed chemically cannot be returned to the original form by simply mechanical means.

As stated, heat, light or electrical ENERGY accompany any chemical change. When some materials combine they release heat. Cheap, abundant materials which do this are used as fuels. (NUCLEAR REACTORS also produce heat, but this represents nuclear, not chemical change.)

Light energy is utilized in other reactions such as PHOTOSYNTHESIS, where water and carbon dioxide combine to form sugar. Assisting in this reaction is CHLOROPHYLL. Chlorophyll is needed for the reaction to occur, but doesn't enter into the reaction. Such a material is a catalyst. CATALYSTS are necessary to promote certain chemical changes.

LIGHT energy is used to take a picture. The light causes chemicals on the film to change. These chemicals react in a way which preserves the pattern of light reflected from the subject. In this reaction again, energy in the form of light, is absorbed.

If a chemical reaction proceeds slowly, or the materials involved are in small quantities, the energy change may not be apparent. An energy change accompanying a rusting nail is difficult to see. However, the energy release from "sparklers" or skyrockets is easily recognized.

Chemists classify chemical changes into four groups. One type, for instance, is il-

lustrated by the burning of coal. Coal is primarily made of carbon. Carbon atoms combine with oxygen atoms to form compounds of carbon monoxide or carbon dioxide.

An equation or "chemical sentence" which describes briefly what happens in a chemical reaction, uses symbols or abbreviations for the materials involved. An equation showing the above carbon reaction is $2C + O_2 \rightarrow 2CO$. This type of change is called *combination*.

A second class of chemical change can be illustrated in the breakdown of water molecules. A process called ELECTROLYSIS, using electricity to promote the change, breaks down water molecules to produce oxygen and hydrogen gases. An equation showing this reaction is $2H_2O \rightarrow 2H_2 + O_2$. This type of reaction is *decomposition*.

A third kind of chemical change takes place when an atom or molecule replaces another in a compound solution such as copper sulfate. The iron changes place with the copper, and the copper which is set free can be seen. The equation showing this is $Fe$ (iron) $+ CuSO_4$ (copper sulfate) $\rightarrow FeSO_4 + Cu$. This type is *replacement*.

In the fourth type, two compounds break down to exchange their parts. This happens for example when sodium chloride (table salt) and silver nitrate react, forming silver chloride and sodium nitrate. $NaCl + AgNO_3 \rightarrow AgCl + NaNO_3$. This is called a *double replacement* reaction.

All nature is involved in a maze of chemical reactions.                    D. J. I.

SEE ALSO: CHEMISTRY, HEAT OF REACTION, NUCLEAR SCIENCE

**Chemical laws** see Chemistry

**Chemical warfare** Chemical warfare is the military use of chemicals. These chemicals produce gas, fire, and smoke screens to injure or confuse people. Soldiers are trained to use gas masks and other devices to protect themselves against chemical warfare.

Chemical warfare dates back to 429 B.C., when the Spartans of Greece tried to suffocate their enemies by burning wood, pitch, and sulfur. However, rain put out the fire. A few years later the Spartans drove back their enemies by producing fumes of

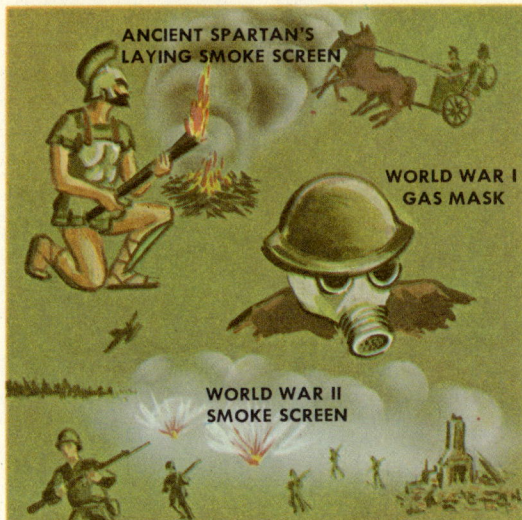

ANCIENT SPARTAN'S LAYING SMOKE SCREEN

WORLD WAR I GAS MASK

WORLD WAR II SMOKE SCREEN

boiling pitch, charcoal, and sulfur.

In 1915 the Germans used CHLORINE gas against the French and English troops, thus opening the era of modern chemical warfare. Later in World War I both the Allied Forces and the Germans made extensive use of gas warfare. Mustard gas, which caused slow-healing burns, was responsible for the greatest number of chemical warfare casualties in World War I.

Both the Allied and other powers of World War II maintained huge stockpiles of gas weapons. Since each side feared reprisals, no attempt was made to use the gas.

In World War II chemical smoke screens were used on the battlefields and seas. These smoke screens hid the movement of troops and ships and were effective in landing actions. Smoke was beneficial in blinding and confusing the enemy. Colored smoke was employed for signals.

Fire was used in many forms during World War II. Attacking soldiers fired flame throwers to burn out enemy gun positions and pill boxes. Incendiary BOMBS containing magnesium, oil, jellied gasoline, or thermite were dropped by airplanes. These bombs scattered hot flames over a wide area. Phosphorus bombs were very destructive, as were the thermite bombs, which burned through steel.

Soldiers in the United States are trained in the use of protective clothing, first-aid, and gas masks. The Chemical Corps has special instruments to detect gas. The Lopair device detects small drops of liquid gas as far as a quarter of a mile away. The *aerosoloscope* counts minute particles of gas in the air.                    P. F. D.

**Chemistry** (KEM-iss-tree) Chemistry is the science that deals with what the earth and the universe are made of. Except for empty space, the material of the universe is called *matter*. Chemistry is the science of what matter contains and how matter changes. The chemist experiments with matter to make useful things for man. The chemist's efforts have sometimes changed the course of history. The manufacturer, the doctor, and even the astronomer depend upon his work. To understand all matter and its changes is the object of chemistry.

Chemistry was used by man even before the year 1 A.D. Its roots lie in two basic interests—man's natural curiosity about his surroundings, and his early attempts to make things such as salt and vegetable dyes. Because man in early times did not use scientific methods, little progress was made toward making chemistry a science for about two thousand years.

Modern chemistry, as a science, truly began during the latter half of the 18th century. Three important ideas set off this new view from the first crude beginnings. There are: (1) the belief in fixed, characteristic properties of matter; (2) a need to relate the behavior of matter to its basic makeup; (3) increasing attention to the "how much" approach to chemical study, through MEASUREMENT and MATHEMATICS.

Today chemistry has become more and more mixed with physics, which also deals directly with the structure and behavior of matter. Physicists are more interested in energy, while chemists concentrate upon the structure and changes of matter.

## THE ELEMENTS
### (Arranged in order of atomic numbers)

| ATOMIC NUMBER | ELEMENT | SYMBOL | ATOMIC WEIGHT | ATOMIC NUMBER | ELEMENT | SYMBOL | ATOMIC WEIGHT | ATOMIC NUMBER | ELEMENT | SYMBOL | ATOMIC WEIGHT | ATOMIC NUMBER | ELEMENT | SYMBOL | ATOMIC WEIGHT |
|---|---|---|---|---|---|---|---|---|---|---|---|---|---|---|---|
| 1 | Hydrogen | H | 1.0078 | 27 | Cobalt | Co | 58.94 | 53 | Iodine | I | 126.92 | 79 | Gold | Au | 197.2 |
| 2 | Helium | He | 4.002 | 28 | Nickel | Ni | 58.69 | 54 | Xenon | Xe | 131.3 | 80 | Mercury | Hg | 200.61 |
| 3 | Lithium | Li | 6.940 | 29 | Copper | Cu | 63.57 | 55 | Cesium | Cs | 132.91 | 81 | Thallium | Tl | 204.39 |
| 4 | Beryllium | Be | 9.02 | 30 | Zinc | Zn | 65.38 | 56 | Barium | Ba | 137.36 | 82 | Lead | Pb | 207.22 |
| 5 | Boron | B | 10.82 | 31 | Gallium | Ga | 69.72 | 57 | Lanthanum | La | 138.90 | 83 | Bismuth | Bi | 209.00 |
| 6 | Carbon | C | 12.00 | 32 | Germanium | Ge | 72.60 | 58 | Cerium | Ce | 140.13 | 84 | Polonium | Po | 210.0 |
| 7 | Nitrogen | N | 14.008 | 33 | Arsenic | As | 74.91 | 59 | Praseodymium | Pr | 140.92 | 85 | Astatine | At | 211 |
| 8 | Oxygen | O | 16.0000 | 34 | Selenium | Se | 78.96 | 60 | Neodymium | Nd | 144.27 | 86 | Radon | Rn | 222.0 |
| 9 | Fluorine | F | 19.00 | 35 | Bromine | Br | 79.916 | 61 | Promethium | Pm | 147 | 87 | Francium | Fr | 223 |
| 10 | Neon | Ne | 20.183 | 36 | Krypton | Kr | 83.7 | 62 | Samarium | Sm | 150.43 | 88 | Radium | Ra | 226.1 |
| 11 | Sodium | Na | 22.997 | 37 | Rubidium | Rb | 85.48 | 63 | Europium | Eu | 152.0 | 89 | Actinium | Ac | 227.1 |
| 12 | Magnesium | Mg | 24.32 | 38 | Strontium | Sr | 87.63 | 64 | Gadolinium | Gd | 156.9 | 90 | Thorium | Th | 232.12 |
| 13 | Aluminum | Al | 26.97 | 39 | Yttrium | Y | 88.92 | 65 | Terbium | Tb | 159.2 | 91 | Protactinium | Pa | 231.04 |
| 14 | Silicon | Si | 28.06 | 40 | Zirconium | Zr | 91.22 | 66 | Dysprosium | Dy | 162.46 | 92 | Uranium | U | 238.14 |
| 15 | Phosphorus | P | 31.02 | 41 | Niobium | Nb | 92.91 | 67 | Holmium | Ho | 164.94 | 93 | Neptunium | Np | 237 |
| 16 | Sulfur | S | 32.06 | 42 | Molybdenum | Mo | 96.0 | 68 | Erbium | Er | 167.2 | 94 | Plutonium | Pu | 239 |
| 17 | Chlorine | Cl | 35.457 | 43 | Technetium | Tc | 99 | 69 | Thulium | Tm | 169.4 | 95 | Americium | Am | 241 |
| 18 | Argon | A | 39.944 | 44 | Ruthenium | Ru | 101.7 | 70 | Ytterbium | Yb | 173.04 | 96 | Curium | Cm | 242 |
| 19 | Potassium | K | 39.10 | 45 | Rhodium | Rh | 102.91 | 71 | Lutetium | Lu | 175.0 | 97 | Berkelium | Bk | 245 |
| 20 | Calcium | Ca | 40.08 | 46 | Palladium | Pd | 106.7 | 72 | Hafnium | Hf | 178.6 | 98 | Californium | Cf | 246 |
| 21 | Scandium | Sc | 45.10 | 47 | Silver | Ag | 107.88 | 73 | Tantalum | Ta | 180.88 | 99 | Einsteinium | E | 255 |
| 22 | Titanium | Ti | 47.90 | 48 | Cadmium | Cd | 112.41 | 74 | Tungsten | W | 183.92 | 100 | Fermium | Fm | 255 |
| 23 | Vanadium | V | 50.95 | 49 | Indium | In | 114.8 | 75 | Rhenium | Re | 186.31 | 101 | Mendelevium | Mv | 257 |
| 24 | Chromium | Cr | 52.01 | 50 | Tin | Sn | 118.70 | 76 | Osmium | Os | 190.2 | 102 | Nobelium | No | 253 |
| 25 | Manganese | Mn | 54.93 | 51 | Antimony | Sb | 121.76 | 77 | Iridium | Ir | 193.1 | 103 | Lawrencium | Lw | 257 |
| 26 | Iron | Fe | 55.85 | 52 | Tellurium | Te | 127.61 | 78 | Platinum | Pt | 195.23 | | | | |

## BASIC CHEMICAL STRUCTURE

Perhaps the most fundamental idea in chemistry is that of the *pure substance*. This is a sample of matter which has the same properties throughout; that is, each part behaves the same as every other part. Pure substances may exist in two forms, as an ELEMENT or a COMPOUND.

An *element* is one form of the simplest possible kind of matter that can exist as such. The smallest possible particle of an element is an ATOM. For chemical purposes all atoms of any one element may be considered to be alike, although physically different kinds of atoms of the same element may exist. These different physical forms of the same element's atoms are called ISOTOPES, and the difference is one of weight. There are 103 recognized chemical elements, and all the world is made from these basic building blocks. Of these 103 different kinds of atoms, perhaps 50 are considered important from the standpoint of availability.

Chemists are accustomed to classifying the elements in terms of their positions upon a form of atomic chart called a *periodic table*. First prepared by the Russian chemist, DMITRI IVANOVITCH MENDELEEV, in 1869, and modified many times since then, the periodic table is to the chemist what a world globe is to a geographer. Each element is given a characteristic identifying number, its *atomic number*. Hydrogen, the simplest element, has the number one, and so on through Lawrencium, number 103, which is the most complex.

All atoms are made up of three significant kinds of fundamental particles: *protons, neutrons,* and *electrons*. The protons and the neutrons are bound together in a tight little bundle called a *nucleus*. The electrons, very light particles, carry a negative electrical charge. In the normal atom, there is one ELECTRON circling outside for each PROTON within the nucleus; thus the total positive and negative electric charges balance each other. The normal atom is electrically neutral. When it gains or loses an electron, it becomes an ion.

Chemists once believed that the electrons orbited about the nucleus of the atom similar to the way that various planets in the solar system orbit about the sun, and indeed, many writers described the atom that way. But the latest research requires more careful description. Although the electrons do surround the neucleus, they cannot be thought of as particles in distinct orbits but must be pictured as rather indistinct clouds of negative electrical charges. The electrons surround the nucleus; each has a unit negative electrical charge. The number of electrons always equals the number of protons within the nucleus of that atom.

The atomic number of a given element is the number of protons within the nucleus of that kind of atom. Isotopes of the same element contain the same number of electrons and protons but differ in the number of neutrons contained in the nucleus. The neutrons are neutral and carry no electrical charge. They do not affect chemical properties of the atom.

The nucleus of an atom is indestructible by any chemical process. It may be split, of course, but by methods which are not chemical in approach. These are classified under NUCLEAR SCIENCE. The chemist concerns himself entirely with the electrons whose interactions, in a very real sense, hold the world together.

The electrons in an atom have been found to arrange themselves in definite patterns about the nucleus, some close, others relatively far away from it. In the larger atoms the innermost electrons remain practically untouchable, but the outermost electrons are often freely exchanged with those of other nearby atoms.

### CHEMICAL REACTIONS

The ability of atoms to exchange electrons provides the basis for the most important classification of the elements into *metals* and *nonmetals*. Those elements which tend to *lose* electrons to other atoms are called *metals*, those that tend to *gain* electrons are *nonmetals*. The metals are most commonly found on the left side and the nonmetals on the right side of the periodic table, although exceptions do exist.

The most important practical fact in the behavior of atoms is that atoms may join together (or, as the chemist says, "react") to form even larger structures. They do this by gaining, losing, or sharing electrons. When two atoms thus combine, they are said to be held together by a *chemical bond*. A chemical bond is formed whenever the rearrangement of the electrons is a more stable system than are the arrangements of the original unbound atoms. A *chemical reaction* is the forming or breaking of chemical bonds to produce new substances. All chemical reactions occur because the stability of matter is increased.

When several atoms thus bond together by sharing electrons, neither atom completely losing or gaining them, the resulting structure is called a MOLECULE, and the substance formed by billions of these is a *molecular compound*. On the other hand, an atom may lose or gain one or more electrons completely, forming a particle called an ION. The metallic elements lose electrons to form positive ions; the nonmetals gain them to form negative ions. The ions of opposite charge then may group together in regular, three-dimensional patterns called CRYSTALS. Ordinary table salt is a familiar example of such an *ionic crystalline compound*.

Due to the attraction which always exists between them, molecules, though electrically-neutral, may also group together to form molecular crystals. Table sugar and naphthalene (the latter used in moth crystals) are examples of *molecular crystal compounds*.

A constitutional chemical formula shows not only what atoms are present, but also how many atoms of each are present in each formula unit, as shown by the small numbers. For complex carbon compounds the chemist also makes use of *structural* formulas which, in addition, show the relative positions of the various atoms within the molecule.

Chemists combine formulas into chemical *equations,* a shorthand technique used to

| SOME IMPORTANT METALS (ATOMS TEND TO LOSE ELECTRONS) | SOME IMPORTANT NON-METALS (ATOMS TEND TO GAIN ELECTRONS) |
|---|---|
| Sodium, Na | Fluorine, F |
| Potassium, K | Chlorine, Cl |
| Magnesium, Mg | Oxygen, O |
| Calcium, Ca | Bromine, Br |
| Zinc, Zn | Iodine, I |
| Aluminum, Al | Sulfur, S |
| Iron, Fe | Arsenic, As |
| Lead, Pb | Nitrogen, N |
| Copper, Cu | Hydrogen, H |
| Tin, Sn | Silicon, Si |
| Silver, Ag | Phosphorus, P |
| Gold, Au | |

# SOME IMPORTANT CHEMICAL COMPOUNDS
## BY CLASS OF COMPOUND

**ACIDS:**

Sulfuric acid, $H_2SO_4$
Hydrochloric acid, HCl
Nitric acid, $HNO_3$
Phosphoric acid, $H_3PO_4$
Carbonic acid, $H_2CO_3$
Acetic acid, $H(C_2H_3O_2)$

**BASES:**

Sodium hydroxide, NaOH
Potassium hydroxide, KOH
Calcium hydroxide, $Ca(OH)_2$
Magnesium hydroxide, $Mg(OH)_2$

**SALTS:**

Sodium chloride, NaCl
Sodium sulfate, $Na_2SO_4$
Potassium nitrate, $KNO_3$
Sodium hydrogen carbonate, $NaHCO_3$
Magnesium sulfate, $MgSO_4$
Calcium phosphate, $Ca_3(PO_4)_2$
Copper sulfate, $CuSO_4$

**OXIDES:**

Water, $H_2O$
Carbon dioxide, $CO_2$
Sulfur dioxide, $SO_2$
Calcium oxide, CaO
Aluminum oxide, $Al_2O_3$
Iron oxide, $Fe_2O_3$

**CARBON CHAIN, ORGANIC, COMPOUNDS:**

Ethyl alcohol, $C_2H_5OH$
Table sugar, Sucrose, $C_{12}H_{22}O_{11}$
Grape sugar, Glucose, $C_6H_{12}O_6$
Natural gas, Methane, $CH_4$
Carbon tetrachloride, $CCl_4$
Ethyl ether, $(C_2H_5)_2O$

Soap, $C_{17}H_{35}COONa$
Acetone $(CH_3)_2CO$
Glycerine, $C_3H_5(OH)_3$
Benzene, $C_6H_6$
Acetylene, $C_2H_2$
Formaldehyde, $H_2CO$

STRUCTURAL FORMULA FOR ACETYL-SALICYLIC ACID, SODIUM SALT (COMMONLY CALLED ASPIRIN)

H = Hydrogen
C = Carbon
O = Oxygen

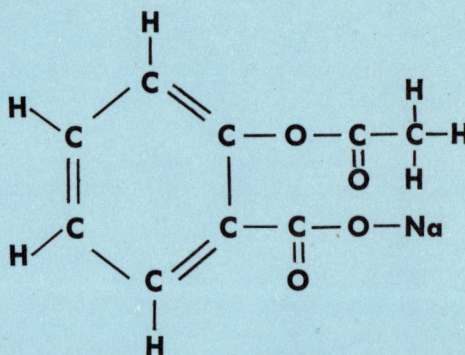

Each line between atoms represents one shared electron pair (one chemical bond)

Note that the structural formula shows the relative position of each atom in the molecule

---

study the course of a chemical reaction. The chemical equation representing the reaction between sulfuric acid and sodium hydroxide is shown below:

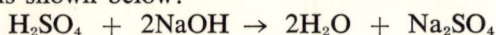

$$H_2SO_4 + 2NaOH \rightarrow 2H_2O + Na_2SO_4$$

sulfuric acid + sodium hydroxide yields water + sodium sulfate

A correct chemical equation must be balanced. This means the total number of atoms on both sides must be equal. Furthermore, not all equations which may be written actually represent true chemical reactions. Only by experiment is it possible to determine which reactions will occur.

## BASIC OPERATIONS OF CHEMISTRY

The chemist's workplace is called a LABORATORY. Here he performs those experiments upon which true scientific knowledge must depend. Modern chemistry has become so complex that it is quite impossible to describe in detail all of a chemist's laboratory work. However there are four classical operations frequently performed in chemical laboratory work. (1) *Solution:* A solid or a liquid is intimately mixed with another liquid so that the molecules or ions of the two substances actually diffuse among each other. (2) *Crystallization:* The desired compound, previously dissolved, is caused to leave the solution and settle on the bottom of the vessel in the form of pure crystals, while the undesired substances (impurities) remain dissolved. (3) *Distillation:* A liquid is carefully heated to convert it into a vapor. The vapor is then passed through a cooled tube and recondensed into a liquid. In this manner substances boiling at different temperatures may be separated. (4) *Quantitative combustion:* A weighed sample of the substance to be examined is burned in an atmosphere of pure oxygen, and the gaseous products formed are absorbed and weighed. Spectrography, ion-exchange, and electrolytic deposition are some other methods widely used by chemists today.

A modern chemistry laboratory

American Oil Co.

### BRANCHES OF CHEMISTRY

Because literally the whole world of matter is subject to chemical study, each chemist has found it necessary to concentrate his attention on one of the many specialized fields of this subject. Some of these specialized *fields* are: (1) *General or Inorganic Chemistry,* which investigates principles and methods applicable to many other fields. (2) *Physical Chemistry* is the theoretical and mathematical study of the chemical reaction itself. Here the chemist and physicist work so closely together that it is often impossible to distinguish their work. (3) *Analytical Chemistry* is the study and practice of methods for determining just what substances are present within a specific quantity of matter, and exactly how much of each is present. (4) *Organic Chemistry* is the study of the carbon chain compounds. (5) BIOCHEMISTRY deals with the compounds and reactions in living organisms. (6) *Pharmaceutical chemistry* is the chemical study of drugs and medicines. (7) *Industrial Chemistry* and *Chemical Engineering* apply chemical principles to the satisfaction of man's material need and comfort. (8) *Geochemistry* considers the chemical aspects of the earth's structure. (9) *Chemical Education* is becoming increasingly important every day. It concerns itself with the teaching of chemistry.     C. F. R.

SEE ALSO: BOHR THEORY, COMPOUND, ELEMENTS, ION, ORGANIC COMPOUNDS, RUTHERFORD THEORY

**Cherry** Cherry trees and shrubs belong to the ROSE family. Cherry flowers have five petals. They are pink or white. Clusters of flowers bloom in spring before the leaves appear.

There are three groups of cherries: sweet, sour, and ornamental.

Sweet cherries are eaten as fresh fruit and sour cherries are eaten as cooked fruit. Most sweet cherry trees grown in the United States are in California, Washington and Oregon.

Sweet cherry tree, fruit and blossom

Flowering cherry trees and shrubs were developed in China and Japan. Some of them are planted near the Lincoln Memorial in Washington, D.C.

Cherry wood is used for making pipes and furniture. A violet dye and prussic acid are made from cherry leaves.     M. R. L.

**Chert** see Rocks

**Chestnut** see Nuts

**Chickadee** The chickadee is a small gray bird with a black cap, black bib, and white cheeks. It has a long tail and a short stubby bill. The chickadee is smaller than a SPARROW. It is a very active BIRD. It can hang upside down as well as right side up when searching for insects.

The bird's name comes from its clear distinct call—*chick-a-dee-dee-dee.* The chickadee does not migrate. It feeds on insects as well as berries and seeds. It makes its nest of moss, fur, and feathers in a hole in a tree, usually a woodpecker's hole. It is partial to forest regions where pines, firs, and cedars grow. The chickadee lays from six to ten eggs. The eggs are white with reddish-brown speckles.

There are numerous species of the chickadee. About 16 species are found in North America, ranging from Newfoundland to Florida and the Gulf of Mexico.     W. J. K.

Chickadee

Mrs. Allan D. Cruickshank

Helen J. Challand

The many varieties of domestic chickens (right) probably came from the wild jungle fowl (left)

**Chicken** A chicken is a tame bird commonly seen on farms. Its flesh and its eggs are used for food. The chicken was first domesticated, or tamed, over 3000 years ago. There are now more than 100 varieties, or kinds, of chickens. They are all believed to have come from a wild *jungle fowl* of southwest Asia.

Modern varieties produce better meat and larger eggs than wild chickens. They have been developed by many years of careful, selective breeding. The Plymouth Rocks, Rhode Island Reds, Leghorns, and New Hampshires are common American varieties. Another variety is the little bantam.

Capons are also raised on poultry farms. A *capon* is a rooster (male) that has had its sex glands (testes) removed. This is called *castration,* and is done when the chicks are 8-10 weeks old. Capons develop hen-like combs and wattles. They are easier to fatten, grow larger, and have more tender meat than normal roosters.          J. C. K.
SEE ALSO: FOWL

**Chicken pox** Chicken pox is a disease of children, although adults can contract it if they have not had it in their childhood. It is very contagious, or catching. It is not related to SMALLPOX although when people were naming this disease—about 1530 A.D.—they thought it was little smallpox. The medical name for the condition is *varicella.*

It attacks the individual first with a mild fever soon followed by an eruption on the face and body.

No germ has been found causing this condition; and it seems to behave like a VIRUS infection. However, no virus has yet been recovered. Chicken pox occurs in epidemics every three or four years. These epidemics usually occur in the very late fall or in the early spring. It is spread from one person to another by the droplet spray from the nose or throat of the one who is sick, and the disease is usually passed to others before the eruption comes out. After the spots are all crusted over, the patient can no longer spread the disease. Most health departments—to whom the disease must be reported—require isolation of the sick person until all the crusts have come off.     H. K. S.

**Chicle** Chicle is used in making chewing gum. It comes from the gum of the tropical, evergreen, *Sapodilla* tree. The Mayan Indians chewed chicle long before America was discovered. The Sapodilla tree grows mainly in Florida, Mexico, and Central America.

The bark of the Sapodilla tree contains a milky substance that is chicle. When the bark is slashed, the chicle oozes out. The chicle is then gathered and boiled down to get rid of most of the water. Then it is formed into blocks and sent to chewing gum factories. Today, about nine-tenths of all chewing gum is produced in the United States.          M. R. L.

**Chicory** (CHICK-uh-ree) Chicory is a small plant which bears white, blue, or pink flowers. The young roots are sometimes cooked in stews but are better known as a substitute for COFFEE. They are sometimes mixed with natural coffee.

**Chicory**

Chicory grows wild in Europe, Asia, and North America. The United States and southern Canada grow chicory as a cultivated plant. It has spreading branches, coarse leaves, and roots that are long, fleshy, and milky.

The pure food laws of the United States stipulate that a mixture of chicory and coffee be labeled as such. In order to discover chicory in coffee, the ground coffee can be mixed in water. The coffee floats and the chicory separates and colors the water.

V. V. N.

**Chigger** see Mite

**Chimpanzee** (tchimm-pan-ZEE) The chimpanzee is an anthropoid APE. Anthropoid means "like man." Its face has an almost human appearance. Its four long fingers and a thumb on each hand make grasping and the handling of objects very easy. Chimpanzees also have "thumbs" instead of big toes on their feet. They have no tails. Chimpanzees sometimes grow as tall as five feet and have been known to weigh up to 160 pounds.

Chimpanzees have been found in Africa from the jungles of French Guinea to Western Uganda and the dark thick jungles of the Congo. They do not like the plains and the open country.

Chimpanzees are *arboreal,* which means "tree-dwellers." Throughout the jungles and forests they travel swinging from limb to limb. As they travel they make a wide

**Chimpanzee**

Courtesy Society For Visual Education, Inc.

variety of sounds. The most common one is a loud, high-pitched cry. For sleeping, chimpanzees build nests high up in trees. The female gives birth to one baby at a time.

The chimpanzee's diet may consist of fruits, buds, bananas, small animals, birds' eggs and insects. Their preference, though, seems to be more for plants rather than animals or animal products.

In captivity the young are very friendly and sociable but as they grow older they become more withdrawn and unsociable, even dangerous. They can and often do develop human-like attachments to man. Chimpanzees live from 20 to 24 years and are of special interest to scientists because of their striking similarity to man. They are curious, imitative and appear to have a keener problem-solving ability than any other animal known to man. Mechanical skills can be developed in them and their sense of rhythm is very strong. In tests of intelligence they have been known to compare favorably with three-year-old children. They can be taught to master such tasks as eating with a spoon, a knife and a fork. Because of their great similarities to man it is possible that they might serve well as substitutes for man in scientific experimentation and research.

G. A. D.

**Chinch bug** see Bugs

**Chinchilla** The chinchilla is a small rodent found in the mountain areas of South America. It is about ten inches long and has large ears and a bushy tail. It is covered with a soft, thick, silver-gray fur.

The chinchilla is a very shy and timid creature. It hastily retreats to a hiding place at the sound of the least disturbance. It feeds on plants, fruits, grains, and roots. It uses its front paws to hold the food.

The FUR of the chinchilla is very beautiful and valuable. It is one of the softest, most delicate and luxurious of all furs. It is more valuable than sable. The wild chinchilla is gradually becoming extinct. It has been hunted and killed for its valuable fur. Today the chinchilla is being raised on farms for commercial purposes. A full length coat requires about 120 pelts.

W. J. K.

SEE ALSO: RODENTIA

**Chipmunk**

**Chipmunk** The chipmunk is a rodent often called a *ground squirrel*. It has cheek pouches for carrying food. Its back is marked by light and dark stripes. Its tail is flat and feather-like. It is a very lively, noisy, and amusing creature. It lives at the edges of forests and rocky areas.

The chipmunk digs long burrows beneath logs, stumps, or rocks. These burrows often consist of many connected compartments and are used by successive generations of chipmunks. In the fall the little creatures keep very busy gathering supplies of nuts, seeds, and grains as winter food. The chipmunk is a hibernating animal although occasionally it comes out on warmer days.

A familiar species of chipmunk in the western part of the United States is known as the *Eutamias*. It is smaller than the chipmunk found in the eastern sections. The chipmunk adjusts successfully to captive life, particularly if taken very young and given reasonable care.                    W. J. K.

SEE ALSO: RODENTIA

**Chitin** (KI-tin) Chitin is the horny substance found in the shells of CRABS, outer coverings of insects, and hard parts of similar creatures and some plants. Pure chitin is a white powder which is very difficult to dissolve.

The chemical structure of chitin is similar to that of CELLULOSE. Both substances consist of many SUGAR molecules which are attached one to the other in a long chain. Even though chitin and cellulose are composed of sugar they do not act anything like sugar since neither chitin nor cellulose can be digested by man.

There are a number of chemically treated chitin products now being used in many industries. Recently the drug, cosmetic and textile industries have been using modified chitin products as thickeners and protective coatings.

A general formula for chitin is $C_{30}H_{50}N_4O_{19}$, for which the molecular weight is 770.73.                    M. S.

SEE ALSO: CARBOHYDRATES, INSECTA

**Chiton** (KYE-tuhn) A chiton is a small mollusk that has eight valves to its shell, one foot, and no eyes. The valves are the sections of its shell. They overlap one another as do the shingles on a house. Underneath the shell the animal's body is very soft. Most of the body is a large powerful foot which helps the chiton move.

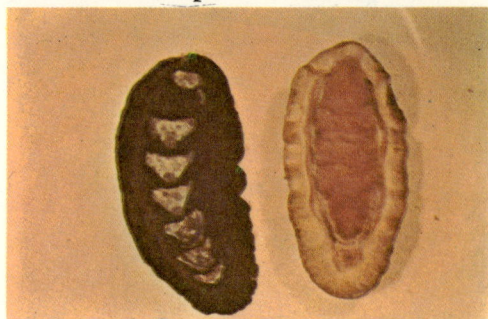

**The chiton is found in rock pools at the seashore**

This primitive mollusk has the basic characteristics of the more advanced members of its group. It has a complete digestive system, kidneys, a three-chambered heart, and a ladder-like nervous system. Its insignificant head is merely the narrow forward end of the foot and possesses a mouth but no eyes. The shell of eight calcareous plates is secreted by the mantle. Its diet consists mainly of algae.                    H. J. C.

SEE ALSO: MOLLUSCA

**Chloride** (KLO-ride) A chloride is a compound made by CHLORINE in combination with certain other elements.

The chlorides, especially the common ones like sodium chloride—common table salt—are a useful family of compounds.

The chlorides are derivatives of HYDRO-CHLORIC ACID. Each chlorine atom in a chloride is in a −1 oxidation state which means it is actually an ION with a negative charge of 1. The test for the presence of the chloride ion in solution is to add silver nitrate. If a white precipitate forms which cannot be dissolved by nitric acid and can be dissolved in ammonium hydroxide, the chloride ion is present.

Sodium chloride is the most important of metallic chloride salts. It is the starting point from which man gets all his SODIUM and chlorine as well as the source of many useful chemicals, among them hydrochloric acid. It is used in food preservation, leather tanning and many other processes.

Other important chlorides are calcium chloride, used to melt ice on roads; titanium tetrachloride which provides smoke for sky-writing; silver chloride, for photographic development; and aluminum chloride, a catalyst in the petroleum and dye-making industries.                                   E. R. B.

SEE ALSO: COMPOUND

## Chlorination see Chlorine, Water

## Chlorine (KLO-reen) Chlorine (C1) is an element which usually occurs as a greenish-yellow gas, two and one-half times as heavy as air. It belongs, along with bromine, iodine, fluorine, and astatine, to a family group of ELE-MENTS called the *halogens*. It has an irritating odor and is poisonous in large quantities. It is useful, however, as a bleach and a germ-killer. Chlorine is never found free in nature but is found combined with other elements, as chloride salts and other compounds.

Chlorine was discovered by the Swedish chemist K. W. Scheele in 1774. He thought he had made an OXIDE, and it wasn't until 1810 that SIR HUMPHRY DAVY proved that it was a new element.

Chlorine is manufactured industrially by ELECTROLYSIS of either a solution of sodium chloride or molten sodium chloride. The chlorine is collected at the positive pole of an electrolytic cell, piped off, and liquefied by compression. It is then shipped in steel tanks. Ocean water and inland salt deposits, which can be treated with water to form salt solutions or BRINE, are sources of chlorine.

Chlorine has an atomic weight of 35.457 and an atomic number of 17. Because of the way the electrons are arranged in the atom, chlorine combines readily with other elements to form hundreds of inorganic and organic compounds.

The many uses of chlorine alone and in compounds make it very important industrially. Over 500,000,000 pounds are used annually in the United States. Its greatest use is as a BLEACHING AGENT. It bleaches very rapidly by a reaction with water, in which oxygen is freed and combines with dyes in paper and cloth to form colorless compounds. This bleaching action can be observed at home by using a weak solution of ink and water and a teaspoonful of liquid laundry bleach as the source of chlorine.

Chlorine is also a powerful germ killer. By oxidation it kills bacteria which cause typhoid and many other diseases. Chlorine is used extensively in treating drinking water (1 drop liquid chlorine in 50 gals. water kills all bacteria), swimming pools, and sewage.

Another important use of chlorine is in the manufacture of other chemicals, principally HYDROCHLORIC ACID. Some of the other chemical products are CARBON TETRA-CHLORIDE, CHLOROFORM, freon gas (used in refrigerators), and coal tar dyes. It is also used in extracting metals from their ores and in purifying oil.                              E. R. B.

## Chloromycetin see Antibiotics

## Chloroform (KLO-ruh-form) Chloroform is a chemical substance composed of carbon, hydrogen and chlorine. It is a clear, colorless liquid with a sweet burning taste and a sharp sweetish smell. Physicians sometimes prescribe it as a medication in the treatment of colic, lockjaw and hydrophobia. One of its best known uses was as a general ANESTHETIC in surgery. As a general anesthetic it must be used very carefully. Despite its many advantages as an anesthetic, it creates side effects which are often very dangerous. Today, other anesthetics have replaced chloroform.

Credit for the discovery of chloroform is shared by three scientists—Soubeiran, Leibig and Samuel Guthrie. Its discovery was made around 1831. The formula is $CHCl_3$.

G. A. D.

## WHY IS CHLOROPHYLL NECESSARY IN PLANTS THAT MAKE FOOD?

**Materials: Plant, alcohol, containers, iodine, aluminum foil**

1. Put a green leaf in a small glass of alcohol. Set this in a larger container of boiling water. Never boil alcohol directly over a flame.
2. After several minutes the alcohol will become green and the leaf white.
3. Test for starch by applying a few drops of iodine to the leaf. It will turn a dark blue if starch is present.
4. Cover one entire leaf on a plant with foil. Permit it to grow for three days.
5. Remove the foil. The leaf has lost some of its green coloring. Test for starch.

**Chlorophyll** (KLOR-uh-fill) Chlorophyll is the green material in plants. Plants are not able to make food without it. Since animals lack chlorophyll, they depend on green plants for food.

Chlorophyll, using the energy from light, can change CARBON DIOXIDE and water into sugar and release oxygen. This process is basic to all food production for living things. A chemical formula for chlorophyll is a combination of these two pigments—$C_{55}H_{72}O_5N_4Mg$ and $C_{55}H_{70}O_6N_4Mg$.

When sunlight or artificial light is not sufficient, the chlorophyll fades out in leaves and permits other colors to show through. This occurs in the fall and gives trees in autumn their beautiful colors. As the sun's rays become less direct, and chlorophyll gradually weakens to reveal red, yellow, and brown pigments.        H. J. C.

SEE ALSO: CARBON CYCLE, PHOTOSYNTHESIS

**Chocolate** see Cocoa

**Cholera** (KAHL-uh-ruh) Cholera is a disease that is caused by a comma-shaped germ. More people have this disease in India and other countries in Asia than in other parts of the world. People who have this disease are very sick and sometimes die. It causes diarrhea, vomiting and loss of weight. It is spread from one person to another by flies, milk, water or food containing the germs. It is also spread by soiled hands. To stop the spread of cholera, people should use boiled water and milk. The food should be cooked. Houses should be screened. People should wash their hands often.

The comma-shaped bacterium, *Vibrio cholerae,* attaches itself to the walls of the intestines. In addition to the other symptoms, the person is unable to eliminate urine. The body temperature drops. The person frequently collapses from shock. Because of the prevalence of cholera in Asia, it is often called *Asiatic* cholera.

Cholera *Morbus* is not caused by any one bacterium. It may be caused by chemical poisoning, sudden chilling of the intestines or by bacterially infected food.

           M. I. L.

**Cholesterol** (kuh-LESS-tuh-rahl) Cholesterol is a fat which is found in the human body and in other large animals. It does not look like other fats which one sees on meat in a butcher shop. Cholesterol in its pure form is a white material which looks like sugar or salt. It is made up of tiny CRYSTALS which can be seen under the microscope.

The cholesterol of the body is found in fatty tissues, but especially in the brain, spinal cord, and nerve tissue. It is also found in fatty foods such as egg yolk, dairy products, solid shortenings, and cooking fats made from animal fat. Corn oil and peanut oil are also fats, but they come from vegetables and do not contain cholesterol.

For laboratory and other uses pure cholesterol is obtained from the spinal cord of cattle. It is also found in large amounts in wool grease or LANOLIN. It is probably the cholesterol content more than anything else which has made lanolin so popular in beauty and healing creams. Also, cholesterol-containing lotions are reported to have a soothing effect on irritated skin.

In addition to the normal places where cholesterol is found in the body, it is also found in gallstones and sometimes too much of it is found in the blood. Scientists are still trying to find out whether or not too much cholesterol in the blood can cause hardening of the arteries and heart disease. However, there is proof that using peanut or corn oil instead of butter for cooking will lower the amount of cholesterol found in the blood.

The chemical formula for pure cholesterol is $C_{27}H_{46}O$. The molecular weight is 386.64. Vitamin D and certain HORMONES of the body have chemical formulas similar to cholesterol.      M. S.

**Chordata** (kohr-DAY-tuh) A cloth tent will fall down unless it is held up with stiff poles. In the same way, the soft bodies of people are held up with strong inner skeletons. People belong to a large group of animals called *Chordates* which means, "with a cord."

At some time during their lives, all chordates have a *notochord* or "back cord." This is a stiff, elastic rod which runs along the back. It allows the animal to bend from side to side and keeps the body from folding like an accordian.

As a child grows taller, he needs stronger bones to hold a larger body. Many of the large chordates develop a stronger backbone made of small bones, called *vertebrae*. Just as a coiled rod bends more easily than a straight rod, the vertebrae allow the animal to bend and twist more easily. Mammals, birds, fish, reptiles, and amphibians are chordates with backbones made of vertebrae. They are known as *vertebrates*.

But some chordates are small and poorly developed. If a person walks along the ocean beach at low tide, he will find the lower chordates. He may be squirted by the small *tunicate,* which attaches itself to a rock and draws food through a funnel. He will have to dig in the wet sand to find the *acorn worm* and *amphioxus.* In these animals, the notochord is the only skeleton. Some of them lose the notochord as they become adults. These animals are often called *invertebrate* chordates or chordates "without vertebrae."

Although the chordates make up in numbers of species less than 1% of the animal kingdom, this phylum is one of the most interesting. It contains man and many of the animals important to man. Some of the most progressive animals are found among the chordates. Since they have explored every type of environment, they are found on land, in sand and mud, on rocks, in fresh and salt water and in the air. Many have powerful muscles and paired appendages, so that they can travel great distances at high speed. With strong supporting skeletons, some grow to tremendous size. The blue whale, for example, reaches a length of over 100 feet.

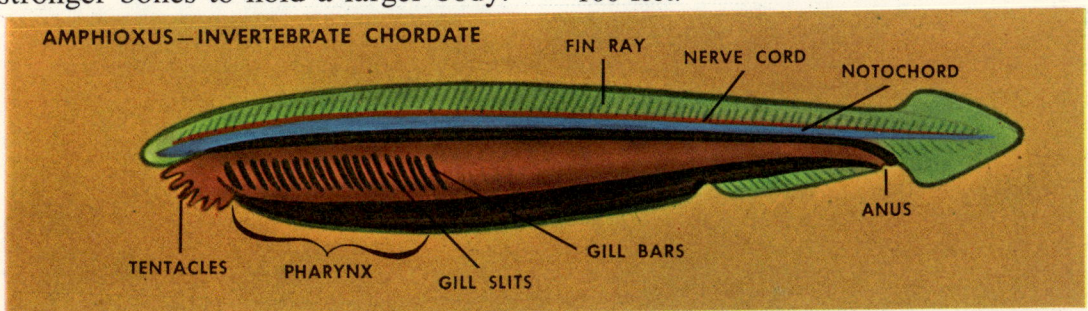

AMPHIOXUS—INVERTEBRATE CHORDATE

FIN RAY    NERVE CORD    NOTOCHORD    ANUS    GILL BARS    GILL SLITS    PHARYNX    TENTACLES

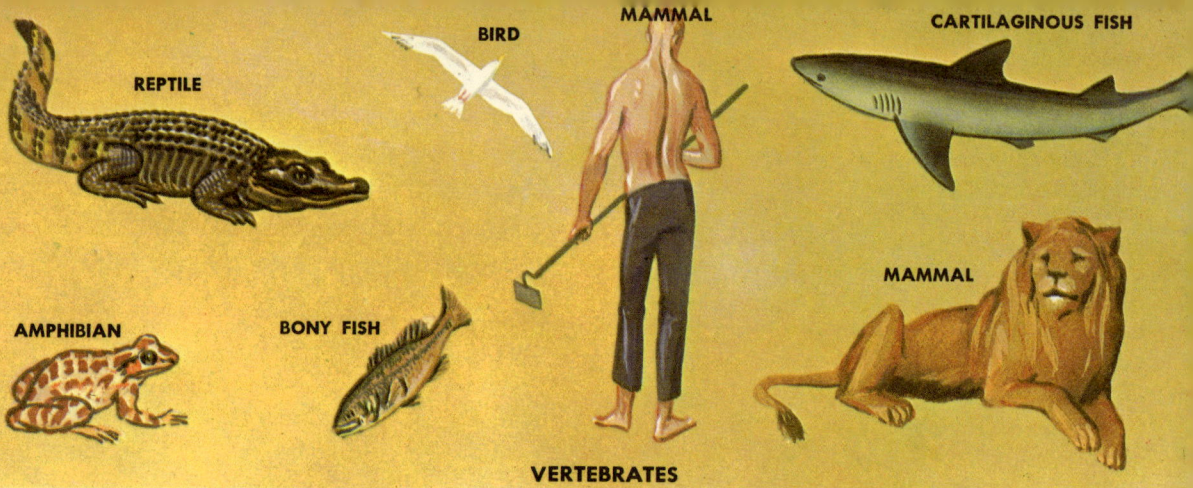

REPTILE    BIRD    MAMMAL    CARTILAGINOUS FISH    MAMMAL    AMPHIBIAN    BONY FISH

VERTEBRATES

The chordates are also distinguished by having a long, hollow, nerve cord, which extends the length of the back. Among some of the vertebrates with a distinct head, the nerve cord is enlarged to form a BRAIN.

At some time during their development, all chordates have *gill slits*. These open through the sides of the pharynx, or cavity between the mouth and the opening to the digestive tract. A continuous channel extends from the mouth to the pharynx to the exterior. Among aquatic animals, like the lower chordates, lamprey eel, and fish, the gill slits are used for breathing throughout adult life. However, in air-breathing animals, the gills appear only in the embryo. As the animal develops, LUNGS pouch out from the pharynx and replace the gills as a means of breathing. Rarely do lungs and gills appear at the same time.

## CHORDATES WITHOUT SKULLS

Although there are many classes of chordates, there are really two main divisions. The *acraniates* are without a cranium or skull, since they have no head. They also lack vertebrae and appendages for locomotion. Included in this group are the primitive marine chordates, the acorn worms, tunicates and amphioxi. As adults, they closely resemble the invertebrates.

The tiny marine acorn worm looks very much like an earthworm. Behind a long snout or proboscis, which is used for burrowing in the sand, there is a short thick collar, followed by a long trunk. The mouth is located on the bottom surface, at the point where the collar and snout are joined. Extending from the collar into the snout is the short, poorly-developed notochord, which supports the proboscis.

Common on ship bottoms, wharves, and other firm surfaces are the tunicates with their sac-like bodies. These animals surround themselves with a covering or tunic of cellulose, a substance common to the plant kingdom. The free-swimming LARVA, which looks like a tadpole has a well-developed notochord in the tail as well as a primitive brain. However, it cements itself to a hard surface and becomes transformed. The tail, nerve cord, brain, and notochord disappear. Through two siphons, raised on the sides of the body, foods enter and wastes are eliminated.

Another sand-burrower is the small, slender, fish-shaped amphioxus, or lancelet. The word *Amphioxus* really means, "pointed at both ends." Since it has a highly developed, segmented body, this animal closely relates to the vertebrates. For the first time, the muscles appear in tiny bundles, called *somites*. A notochord, which extends the length of the body, remains throughout life.

## CHORDATES WITH SKULLS

The *Craniata,* or *Vertebrata,* make up the second main chordate division. Since these animals have a head, there is a cranium, or skull, which houses the brain. For locomotion, they have well-developed fins, limbs or wings. Although the notochord appears in the embryo, it is later surrounded by the vertebrae, in the adult animal. Among higher vertebrates, the notochord is replaced completely by the vertebrae.

The FISH or *Pisces,* make up the large group of aquatic vertebrates. Included with the eel-shaped jawless fish, are the hagfish and lampreys. For these animals, the head end forms a funnel-shaped sucker and the notochord remains throughout life.

The cartilaginous fish, like the SHARK, SKATE and RAY, develop a vertebral column and a skeleton of cartilage. Nearly half of all vertebrate species are made up of the scaly-skinned bony fish which develop a strong skeleton, consisting mainly of bone.

Included among the four-legged verte-brates, or *tetrapods,* are the amphibians, reptiles, birds (Aves) and mammals. While a few like the sea turtle are aquatic, most tetrapods live on land. Although some, like the NEWT and SALAMANDER retain their gills as adults, even these animals breathe with lungs.

Chordates reach the highest level of development. With bilateral symmetry, a distinct head and tail region appear. With three body layers, chordates have well-developed organ systems. Reproduction is sexual and each individual has a pair of reproductive organs.      E. P. L.
SEE ALSO: AMPHIBIANS, BIRD, PISCES, REP-TILIA, MAMMALIA

**Choroid coat**   see Eye

**Chromatic**   see Lens, man-made

**Chromatophores**     (KROH-mah-tuh-fohrz) Chromatophores are cells which, by changing shapes, cause variations in the skin color of certain fish, amphibians, and some invertebrates.
SEE: SQUID

**Chromium** Chromium is a hard, brittle, steel-gray metal which is obtained from *chromite*. Its name comes from the Greek word *chroma* meaning "color." Chromite is mined mainly in Turkey, the Soviet Union, Southern Rhodesia, South Africa and New Caledonia.

Chromium was discovered in 1798 by L. N. Vauquelin and M. H. Klaproth who were working independently. Its atomic number is 24, and its atomic weight is 52.01. Its high melting point, 1930° C, makes it valuable in making airplane engines, safes, armor plate and high speed tools.

Since chromium is also rust-resistant, it is used to plate metals. The automobile industry uses chromium for radiators, pistons, valves, shafts, bearings, and decorative trim. Stainless steel for knife blades, which must be rustproof, is made by adding 16–18% chromium to steel.

The United States government uses chromium-plated steel engravings for printing money and postage stamps.     V. B. I.
SEE ALSO: ELEMENTS

**Chromosomes** Chromosomes are tiny thread-like parts of a CELL, which can be seen under a high-powered microscope. They are thought to be made up of smaller particles called GENES. These chromosomes and genes are important in determining the HEREDITY of a plant or animal. The process of heredity causes an animal to resemble his ancestors and parents.

Chromosomes appear as dark, elongated pieces inside the *nucleus* of the cell when it is treated with special stains. They vary in shape and often in number, depending upon the species of the particular plant or animal. For example, all the cells of corn plants have twenty chromosomes; all Siamese cats, sixteen; all bullfrogs, twenty-six; all humans, forty-six.

Chromosomes always occur in pairs, thus man has twenty-three pairs. On a pair of duplicate chromosomes are paired genes, thus, not one but two genes called *alleles* control each hereditary factor.

In man the genes controlling sex are on the so-called X-chromosome. All egg (female) cells contain X-chromosomes. Half of the male sperm cells contain an X-chromosome and half have a Y-chromosome. If two X-chromosomes come together in a fertilized egg, a female is born. If an egg is fertilized by a sperm containing a Y-chromosome a male is born.     V. V. N.

**Chronometer**   see Clocks

**Chrysalis**   see Metamorphosis

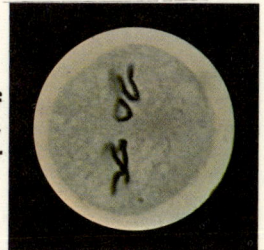

**During the cleavage of a fertilized Ascaris egg, the chromosomes become clearly visible**
Photo-micrograph by National Teaching Aids, Inc.

**Web arrangement of 22 chromosomes in a bug and star pattern of 8 chromosomes in a parasitic hookworm**

**Chrysanthemum**

**Cineraria**

**Chrysanthemum** (krih-SANTH-uh-mum) Chrysanthemums are plants grown for flowers that bloom in the late summer and fall. *Chrysanthemum* means "golden flower." The first ones were a gold color. Today, the flowers come in many other colors. The heads may be smaller than a silver quarter, or larger than a baseball. The leaves are usually strong smelling and coarse.

Chrysanthemums are HERBS that belong to the *composite* family. They should be grown in well-drained garden soil. Chrysanthemums like sunshine, and need thorough watering. Plants are raised by cutting off the new shoots of older plants. These cuttings should be placed in moist sand until new growth appears. Young plants can be put in the garden or in pots.

Chrysanthemums include flowers called daisies, feverfews, marguerites, and pyrethrum. Many kinds of chrysanthemums have been developed in China and Japan. Some existed over 3,000 years ago.     M. R. L.
SEE ALSO: COMPOSITE FLOWER

**Cicada** see Bugs, Insecta

**Cilia** Cilia are hair-like processes of protoplasm which occur on the surfaces of some cells. Their vibrations direct the movements of particles in the body fluid or actually serve as a means of locomotion for the animal.

**Cineraria** (sin-uh-RARE-ee-uh) The cineraria is a flowering plant. It is usually grown indoors or in the greenhouse. This bushy plant grows from one to two and one-half feet tall. The leaves are very large and feel like velvet. The flowers look like small daisies. They may be in bright colors of blue, pink, purple, red, and white. When in bloom the many flowers hide the leaves of the plant.

*Cineraria* is the Latin word for ashes, which describes the ash-gray color of the lower leaves. The cineraria is an HERB that comes from the Canary Islands. This tender plant should be grown in a cool room.

Seeds planted indoors in May will bloom during the fall and winter. They thrive in moist, sandy, loam. Cinerarias are susceptible to two diseases, rust and downy mildew.
    M. R. L.
SEE ALSO: BLIGHT, MILDEW

**Cinnabar** (SIN-uh-bahr) Cinnabar is the only important ore from which MERCURY is obtained. Cinnabar is red sulfide of mercury. Its formula is HgS. A pigment called *vermillion* is made from this bright-red ore. Fine hard grades of cinnabar are carved and polished for use as gems.

**Cinnamon** (SIN-uh-mun) The true cinnamon plant is an evergreen shrub that is native to Ceylon. A light colored and flavored spice is obtained from the plant. It is widely used in South America and Europe.

The "cinnamon" used in the United States is really from the *Cassia* plant. It is often called "Chinese cinnamon" because the plant is native to China. The cassia and true cinnamon plants are separate species of the LAUREL family. In harvesting both plants, shoots are allowed to grow and the bark is removed in long strips. These strips dry and curl to become what is known as "cinnamon bark."     M. R. L.

**Circle** see Earth, Geometry

**Circuits, parallel and series** see Electricity

AORTA   HEART

DORSAL VESSEL

In a grasshopper, blood flows out of the open system and freely bathes the tissues. It has a one-chambered heart

PERICARDIUM    HEART

ABDOMINAL ARTERY

The crayfish also has an open system but with a two-chambered heart. Arteries open into body cavities called sinuses

The frog has a closed system and a three-chambered heart

CAROTID ARCH

CONUS ARTERIOSUS

AURICLES

VENTRICLE

POSTERIOR VENA CAVA

DORSAL AORTA

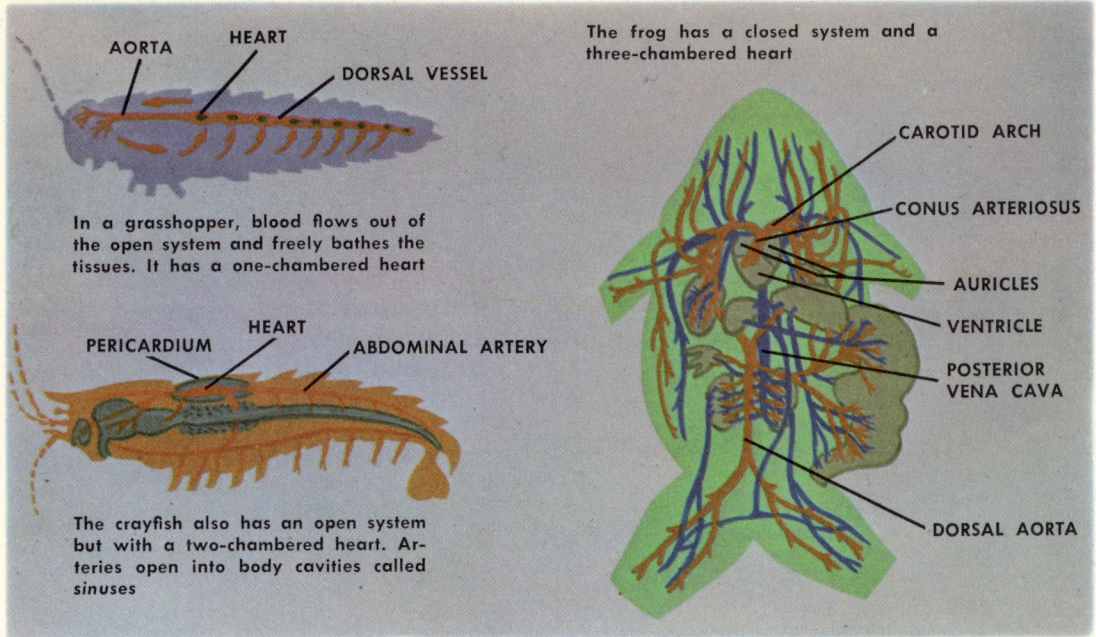

**Circulatory system** The circulatory system and its main organ, the heart, pump, feed, cool, warm, protect, and keep the body well. The HEART is the hardest working organ in the body. It has to squeeze and push, suck and pull steadily, without missing a beat throughout one's whole life.

Attached to every heart in animals from the grasshopper, worm, crayfish, reptile, fish, frog, bird, and finally to man is a system of outgoing and incoming pipes that are called *blood vessels*. These pipes carry food, air, chemicals, water, and enzymes throughout the body to keep it alive and well. The system even has an "army" of billions of white cells to protect it. If the circulatory system breaks or is torn open, it plugs itself automatically with tiny discs called *platelets*. These jam up at the opening to plug the break and are glued together by a substance in the blood called *fibrin*. This is how a scab forms after a cut.

The heart is an amazing engine. It is a pump, designed to keep the BLOOD moving through the circulatory system. It starts working before the body is completely built and works continuously as long as one lives. Every seven seconds the heart pumps two gallons of blood over the circulatory pipe line (a mile long) for every second of every day, even during sleep.

The circulatory system was millions of years in developing. It is important to understand the parts of the body that make blood circulation possible.

First there are *arteries* that carry blood from the heart to the lungs and body. Arteries are present in all circulatory systems. In fact, the first pumping organ was an artery that throbbed.

Then there are *veins,* found only in the later animals. These carry the blood from the lungs and body back to the heart. They are smaller in size than the arteries.

Between these two kinds of "pipes" is a pump called the *heart*. Scientists think that the heart began as a tube that squeezed the blood from a source of concentration out through the whole body. Body organs in simpler forms were fed in much the same way as the land is flooded when a river overflows. The GRASSHOPPER has this type of

## HOW DOES BLOOD CIRCULATE THROUGH THE HEART?

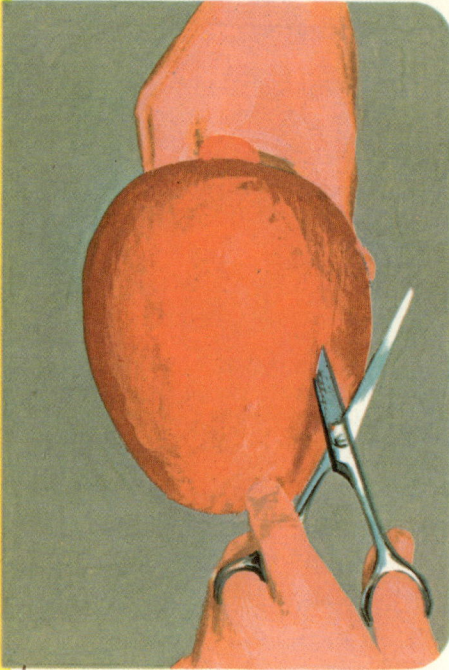

Materials: **Very sharp scissors; razor blade; and a pencil or two; lamb, veal, or pork heart, FRESH**

1 **Find the thick side of the heart—this is the side that pumps to the body.**

2 **The large white vessels at the top are the branches of the aorta. Stick your finger down into one of these vessels, gently probing until you reach the chamber inside.**

3 **Cut with the scissors along the surface of the heart, using the finger as a runner for one point of the scissors. Do the same on the other side and you will have the heart opened up so that you can see for yourself what a marvel of efficiency and perfection it is. Look for the valves; these work steadily and perfectly for years. Can you think of a valve that man has made that is as good?**

4 **With a piece of string trace the flow of blood through the heart.**　　　**L. M.**

circulatory system. In the grasshopper the blood is squeezed along in much the same manner as a swimmer squirting his friends by squeezing his hands in the water.

In the earthworm its blood system is a closed system with ten hearts or lobes (swellings) that do the squeezing (throbbing) and move the blood along. The hearts connect the dorsal and ventral blood vessels. The blood flows toward the anterior end in the dorsal vessel with valves preventing any back flow. Leaving the hearts, the blood is pumped out the ventral vessel in a posterior direction. Other vessels running the length of the earthworm send out lateral branches which go to most of the segments.

The Crayfish found in lakes and ponds, is much bigger and stronger and has many legs, but it cannot leave the water, on which it depends for breathing. Unlike the worm and grasshopper, which breathe air through pores on their bodies, the crayfish breathes through gills. A gill is a breathing apparatus, like lungs, that takes oxygen out of water instead of out of air. The crayfish's gills are in the thorax area. The crayfish also has a new

kind of circulatory system. The simple heart, or throbbing section, has two chambers—one chamber that sucks and a second which pumps. The crayfish's blood system, like that of grasshopper, is an open system.

In the development of circulation, the crayfish was the step before the next major development—the fish.

In fish the heart is a simple one with two chambers that operates in a very large circulatory system.

The fish is a specialized animal, with many organs that need feeding by the blood. It has gills but they are behind its head, inside its body. Its circulation, however, is still in one main direction. The heart receives old blood from the body, pumps it through its two chambers and squirts it out through the second chamber (the ventricle) out through the gills to the body. In the fish's blood, there is also the first mixture of red and white cells.

The frog is the next change in this series. It takes in water through gills during its early life but as an adult breathes air through lungs. Because it needs water to keep its skin

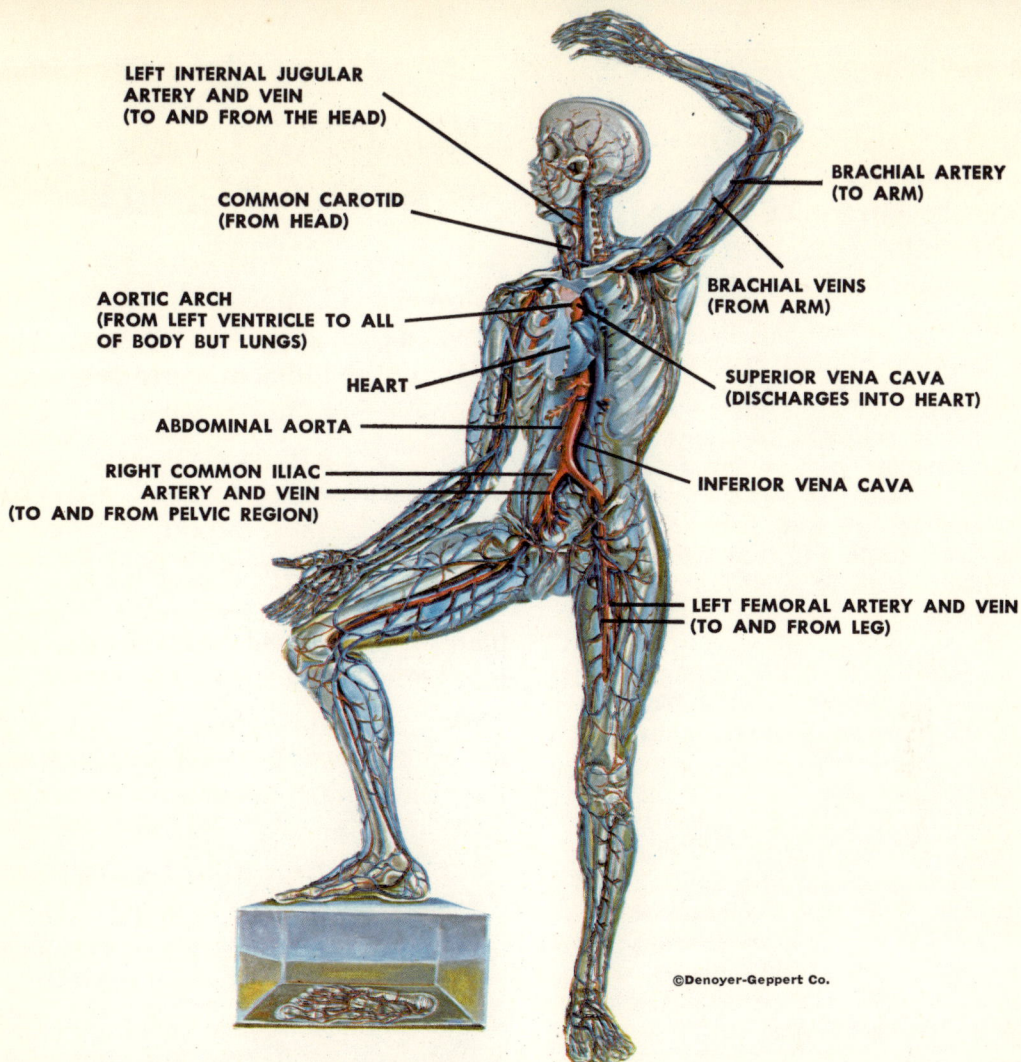

LEFT INTERNAL JUGULAR ARTERY AND VEIN (TO AND FROM THE HEAD)

COMMON CAROTID (FROM HEAD)

AORTIC ARCH (FROM LEFT VENTRICLE TO ALL OF BODY BUT LUNGS)

HEART

ABDOMINAL AORTA

RIGHT COMMON ILIAC ARTERY AND VEIN (TO AND FROM PELVIC REGION)

BRACHIAL ARTERY (TO ARM)

BRACHIAL VEINS (FROM ARM)

SUPERIOR VENA CAVA (DISCHARGES INTO HEART)

INFERIOR VENA CAVA

LEFT FEMORAL ARTERY AND VEIN (TO AND FROM LEG)

©Denoyer-Geppert Co.

wet at all times, the frog cannot leave its damp surroundings for very long. Its circulatory system must adjust to these changes. ·

The frog is quite an improvement on the fish. It has legs and can jump like a grasshopper. And its blood system is a closed circle.

The frog's blood system is really two separate systems that work as one unit. To make this possible, the frog has a three-chambered heart with two auricles (upper chambers) and one ventricle. The three chambers work together to pick up, mix, and circulate two kinds of blood. One kind of blood is called *impure* blood because it contains waste products collected from the body cells and lacks oxygen, having given its supply to these cells. The other kind of blood is called *pure* blood because waste products have been taken out of it, chiefly by the kidneys and lungs, and a new supply of oxygen put into it by the lungs.

The three-chambered heart, while much more efficient than the one or two-cham-

bered hearts, does not function as well as the four-chambered heart occurring in the higher animals and humans. The four chambers compose two separate blood systems, making it possible to feed the organs of the body.

The right side of the heart receives impure blood from the veins and pumps it out to be purified by lungs and kidneys. The left side of the heart then receives the purified blood and pumps it out through the arteries.

In the mammal circulatory system, the gills have now been replaced by lungs. These organs are protected by a cage (the ribs). A new breathing organ, called the *diaphragm,* has been added. All these work together so that one can jump, fight, hunt—literally do everything the animal ancestors could do and more.

Without the four-chambered heart and the blood circulating system attached to it, man could not live for a second.  L. M.

**Circumpolar star** see Constellation, Polaris, Star

**Cirrhosis** (sih-ROE-sis) The liver is an important organ of digestion. Its cells can be injured by infection, by poisonous substances, or by the backflow of bile in the liver following obstruction of the bile ducts. The liver reacts by forming scar tissue. Such a condition is called *cirrhosis*.

There are several types of cirrhosis. The two most common ones are portal cirrhosis and biliary cirrhosis. In *portal cirrhosis* an unusual amount of scar tissue develops following the death of liver cells. Small lumps called *nodules* form along the surface of the organ. The liver may shrink as a result of this increase in scar tissue and cause an impairment of the blood flow to the organ. The blood vessels which join to form the portal vein become congested.

*Biliary cirrhosis* is usually caused by some obstruction which prevents the flow of bile from the liver to the duodenum (the upper part of the intestine). The bile hampered in its normal course spills into the blood stream. When such a condition occurs the body's excrement appears whitish or clay-colored and the skin appears quite jaundiced, or yellow. Obstructions which cause it are often congenital.          G. A. D.

**Cirro-cumulus** see Clouds

**Cirro-stratus** see Clouds

**Cirrus** see Clouds

**Citric acid** (SIT-rick) Citric acid is found in CITRUS FRUITS, especially lemons. Citric acid gives these fruits their sour taste. It plays an important part in the process which gives humans and animals energy and protection against some diseases.

Today citric acid is made by a process which uses certain types of bacteria and a sugar solution, such as molasses. The citric acid made in this way is used in beverages, candy, medicines, foods, and in many chemical processes.

The chemical formula for citric acid is $C_6H_8O_7 \cdot H_2O$.          M. S.

SEE ALSO: ACIDS AND BASES

**Citron** see Citrus fruits

Citronella

**Citronella** Citronella is a fragrant grass cultivated in Asia for its oil. The oil is used in liniment, perfumes, soap, and as a mosquito repellant.
SEE: GRASSES

**Citrus fruits** Citrus fruits are produced by the most important group of tropical and subtropical fruit trees in the world. They grow on evergreen plants and are acid, pulpy fruits. The best known citrus fruits are the lemon, orange, citron, grapefruit, lime, and kumquat. Some other citrus fruits are the limequat, mandarin orange, pomelo, pummelo, shaddock, tangerine, and tangelo. All citrus fruits are rich in Vitamin C.

Citrus fruits are raised commercially in southern Florida, the Mississippi Delta, the lower Rio Grande Valley, and southern California. This area is sometimes called the *citrus belt*. Frost injures all the citrus trees. The lime is the most tender and the kumquat is the hardiest. Citrus fruits will grow best in well-drained soil. For marketing purposes, many trees are planted together in *groves*.

The semi-tropical *lemon* tree is a small, spiny evergreen tree. It grows about fifteen feet tall. Lemon trees have pale green shiny, oval leaves and small flowers of a purplish color. The lemon fruit is about four inches long. It is oblong and has a thick yellow skin. The fruit ripens in the winter but is usually stored until the summer season when there is a great demand for lemon juice for cool drinks.

Commercially, the *orange* is the most important of the citrus fruits. It is the fruit of a long-lived evergreen tree. The orange tree is small and has broad, green leaves. The branches are low, and the flowers are white and wax-like. Because of the beauty and fragrance of the orange blossoms, they have long been worn by brides. Oranges are grown in the citrus belt. There are many varieties. The fruit is round, bright orange in color, and contains a pulp which is divided into oblong segments. These are filled with a sugary and refreshing juice, and in most varieties contain several seeds. Seedless oranges, which are the most popular for eating in the United States, are called *navel* oranges.

The *grapefruit* is a large yellow fruit that grows on the tree in bunches or clusters, as grapes do. It derived its name from this similarity. The grapefruit has an acid, juicy pulp that is in segments like those of an orange. Each grapefruit is from four to seven inches in diameter and weighs one to five pounds. Grapefruit is a popular breakfast food and is used in salads or for its refreshing juice.

The *lime* tree is a small, tropical, thorny evergreen, grown for its strongly acid fruit. The tree grows about eight feet high. Because of its tenderness to frost it is raised only in the southern tip of Florida and California. The fruit of the lime tree resembles the lemon but is green in color.

*Kumquats* grow on shrubby evergreen trees. They are related to the orange and are grown in the citrus belt of the United States. The kumquat tree grows about ten feet tall and has glossy green leaves and small, white, fragrant flowers. The kumquat is a small aromatic fruit about an inch in diameter. Whole kumquats are eaten as fresh fruit, or they are made into jelly and jam. Kumquats are the hardiest of all the citrus fruits.

The *citron* is a large, lemon-like citrus fruit whose thick, spongy peel is candied for use in cakes, candies, and other baked foods. The small, spiny, irregular tree or shrub that bears citron is so tender that its cultivation is limited to southern Florida and California.                    M. R. L.

SEE ALSO: FRUIT TREES, VITAMINS

**Civet** Civets, native to Asia and Africa, are related to cats. The animals have weasel-like faces and gray with black fur. A secretion from special glands is used as a perfume base.

SEE: CAT FAMILY

There are many orange groves in Florida, California and Texas

The oranges grow and ripen

The fruit is picked and put into large baskets or boxes

The oranges are sorted according to size

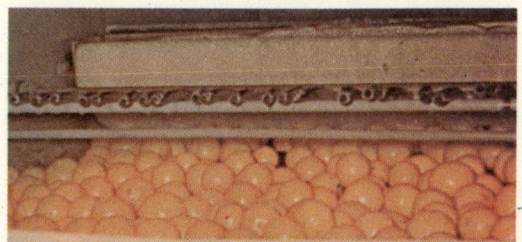

All photos Courtesy Society For Visual Education, Inc.

These oranges are being given a protective coat of wax before shipping

**Horse clam**

**Clam** The clam is a shelled animal which lives in the sea or in fresh water. The soft body is enclosed in a sac which lines two shells. The shells are hinged by a strong muscle which permits the shell to open and close.

The clam has a foot-like organ which it uses to burrow in the sand and mud. It has a siphon of two tubes, one to take in water which supplies the animal with oxygen and food, and the other to expel waste. The fleshy part of the clam is edible.

Clams produce eggs in great numbers. The eggs are fertilized in the water by movable sperm. The sexes may be separate or in the same animal (hermaphroditic.)

Clams live along the Atlantic and Pacific coasts, in the Gulf of Mexico, and in the waters around the British Isles.    W. J. K.

**Class** see Animals, classification of; Plants, classification of

**Claw** A claw is a sharp NAIL on the finger or toe of an animal. It is made of the same material as the fingernails and toenails of a human. Animals use their claws as weapons to protect themselves and to get food.

All members of the CAT FAMILY, such as lions, tigers and the house cat, use their claws when they attack or are attacked.

PARAKEETS use their claws as hooks when climbing on their cages, but BIRDS OF PREY, such as the eagle, use their claws to kill smaller animals for food.    J. K. K.

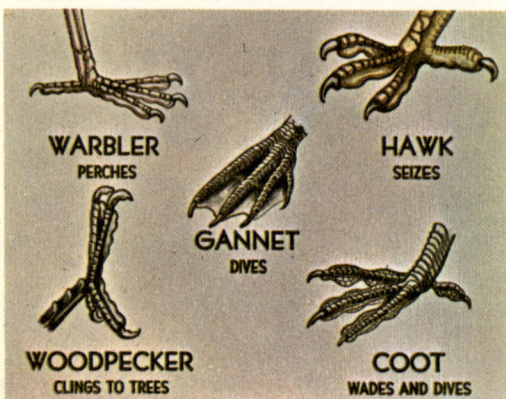

WARBLER
PERCHES

HAWK
SEIZES

GANNET
DIVES

WOODPECKER
CLINGS TO TREES

COOT
WADES AND DIVES

**Clay** Clay is an earthy material made up of fine grains of rock. When moist, clay becomes a slippery, sticky mud that can be shaped easily. Dry clay turns to powder when rubbed together or broken up. Clay becomes hard when fired and is useful in making brick, tile, porcelain, china, earthenware, and drainage pipes. It is also used for filtering and purifying liquids.

Clay consists chiefly of hydrous silicates of ALUMINUM mixed with numerous other substances. The purest kind of clay is white and is called KAOLIN. When there is iron oxide in clay, it is a reddish color. When carbonaceous matter is in it, clay will be grayish.

There are two kinds of clay—residual and sedimentary. *Residual* clay is made when rocks crumble due to the WEATHERING process. *Sedimentary* clay may have been formed in the same way, but the wind or water has carried the clay particles away and deposited them somewhere else. Most clay then has been formed by the crumbling of old rocks or by the grinding action of glaciers.

Different types of clay have special names and uses. Potter's clay and pipe clay are used for inexpensive pottery and pipes. Paper clay is used to give paper a smooth, shiny surface. Fire clay, which can stand high temperatures, is used for firebrick, gas retorts, crucibles and furnace linings. A certain form of fire clay, treated to make it lighter in weight, is important in making missile heads. This clay has been used in the Atlas missile on test runs.    J. K. K.
SEE ALSO: BRICK, ROCKS

**Some uses of clay**

## Cleavage

**Cleavage** (KLEE-vidg) In biology, cleavage is any of the series of divisions by which a fertilized egg develops into a new individual or *embryo*.

The young animal begins life as a fertilized egg. The uniting of the male reproductive cell (sperm) and the female reproductive cell (egg) begins the activity of this new embryo or young animal.

This fertilized egg (ZYGOTE) begins development, but the rate is not the same in all parts. To describe this difference in growth rate, or METABOLISM, certain terms are given for different parts of the egg. The end where concentration of living protoplasm is greatest is called the *animal pole,* while the end where the concentration of food is greatest is called the *vegetal pole*. Natural development is more rapid at the animal pole than at the vegetal pole.

In cleavage the first two divisions, not simultaneously but one following the other, usually cut through the poles of the egg at right angles to each other. The third cleavage cuts the egg between the poles at right angles to the polar axis and a little nearer to the animal pole. All these cleavages result in eight cells, the four at the vegetal end being a little larger than the others.

There are many variations as development continues, but certain general ends are reached even though the manner of attaining them differs in different species of animals. During the latter part of the cleavage period, the cells arrange themselves in the form of a hollow sphere. This is called the *blastula stage*. One side of the blastula moves inward until the walls meet and the embryo is transformed into a double-walled cup or sac called the *gastrula*. The double walls are called germ layers. The outer layer is the *ectoderm;* the inner layer is the *endoderm;* the newly formed cavity is the *primitive gut;* and its opening is the *blastopore*. A middle layer, the *mesoderm,* is eventually formed between the ectoderm and endoderm.

By forming these germ layers, the embryo lays the groundwork for organs. The germ layers continue to develop into various tis-

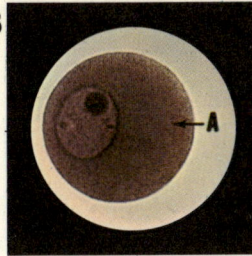

Single-cell stage in a starfish, enlarged 320 times. A is the cytoplasm of the fertilized egg (magnified 320 times)

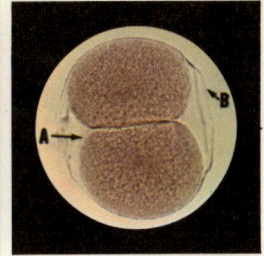

First cleavage of the zygote. A is the divided cell membrane. B, the fertilization membrane, does not divide

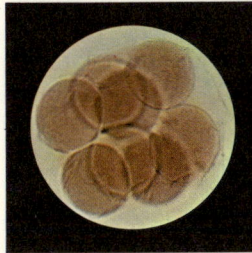

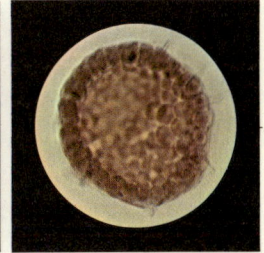

Photo-micrographs by National Teaching Aids, Inc.

Four cells have become eight. The total mass does not change during cleavage

Blastula — the mass has become a hollow ball; differentiation has not started

sues and organs of the body. Each germ layer gives rise to particular organs and tissues.

The ectoderm gives rise to the nervous system, the epidermis, and its derivatives; such as hair, nails, feathers, claws, and hoofs.

The endoderm gives rise to the lining of the digestive and respiratory systems. The glands such as the salivary glands, the liver, and the pancreas are lined with derivatives of the endoderm.

The mesoderm gives rise to the major share of the animal body. Of the mesodermal derivatives, the bones and muscles make up more than half the body weight. The entire circulatory system and lymphatic system (heart, blood, blood vessels, and lymph tubes), the urinary system, the genital organs, the supporting tissues of the digestive and respiratory systems, and the inner layer of the skin are derivatives from the mesoderm.

All embryos are soft delicate structures. They can easily be warped out of shape and deformed if their development is in too rigid an enclosure. They need a soft fluid medium in which to develop. Animals that develop in water have these advantages. In contrast to those that develop in water, embryos that develop from land-type eggs or within the uteri of mammals, form additional structures known as *extraembryonic membranes*. These membranes lie outside the body of the embryo and function as support and protection. They are used only during the embryonic stage and then discarded. V. V. N. SEE ALSO: EMBRYOLOGY

**Cleft palate** Cleft palates come from incomplete development of the roof of the mouth when it is formed before birth. The roof of the mouth and soft palate come from two sections of tissue growing out from the right and left sides. They meet and join in the center. If joining is incomplete, a hole or cleft remains in the roof of the mouth. Speech is difficult and surgigal correction is needed.

Helen J. Challand

**Clematis**

**Clematis** Clematis is a vine with small white or large purple flowers. Some species are HERBS and do not climb. Flowers may be shaped like stars, vases, or bells depending on the species.

**Cliff** A cliff is a nearly vertical rock wall, formed when streams, GLACIERS and ocean waves erode away soft rock in high-lying land and leave hard rock standing.

**Cliff**

**Climate** Climate can be defined as the average weather of any region. These averages need not be for a whole year, but can be figured from data or records for months, weeks, or days. Such averages must be computed from a large amount of data to make them accurate.

Climate is, however, not exactly the same as weather, because WEATHER is the condition of the wind, the rain, sunshine, and temperature in any place at a given time. Changing patterns of wind, rainfall, and sunshine found in a given place over a period of years, is the true meaning of climate.

Climate, of course, is different in different areas. The ancient Greeks' theory of weather was that Earth sloped toward the sun at the equator and sloped away from the sun at the poles. This led them to believe that it was warmer at the equator because it was closer to the sun, and that it was colder at the poles because it was farther away. They still did not know that Earth was tilted on its axis and revolved around the sun.

Modern theories of climate depend on latitude, altitude, and location as to nearness of bodies of water and land areas. In other words, the distance of an area from sea level, its nearness to an ocean or other large body of water, and its nearness to other land masses having a bearing upon the climate of a region. Winds and ocean currents too have a strong affect on climate.

Climate affects the comfort of man. The temperature of skin on the human body is normally about 91.4 degrees Fahrenheit. The upper limit of skin temperature for comfort is about 97 degrees and the lower limit is about 82 degrees. Man can warm the air of cold climates by using fire and wear clothing for protection from cold. In tropical areas all men face some discomfort. Rate of growth is affected by heat. Climate also seems to have an affect on disease. Man's activity seems to be stimulated in cold climate and slowed down in warm climate. In recent years man has tried to control climate. At least he has succeeded in making himself more comfortable in either extreme of climate.

Climate largely determines the kind of vegetation to be found in any area. The two maps show how closely the vegetation zones follow climate zones. For example, the eastern section of the United States is humid with regular rainfall, and is warm in summer, cold in winter. This climate favors deciduous trees, which shed their leaves in winter and lie dormant until spring returns. Grasses thrive in almost any climate, but they are especially suited for the subhumid and semidry areas where rainfall is uncertain. Small, fast-growing spiny plants are adapted to growing in dry areas

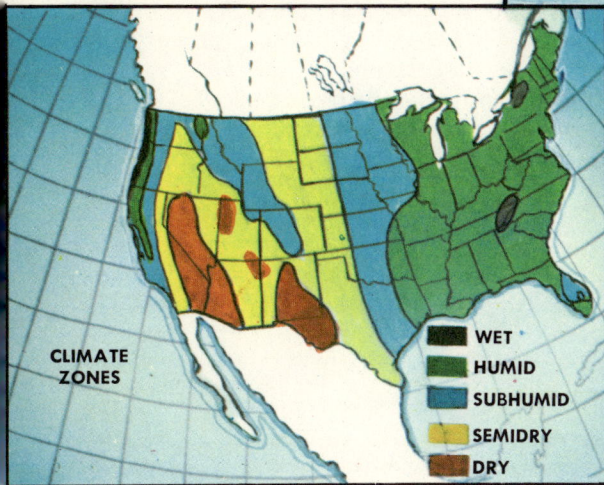

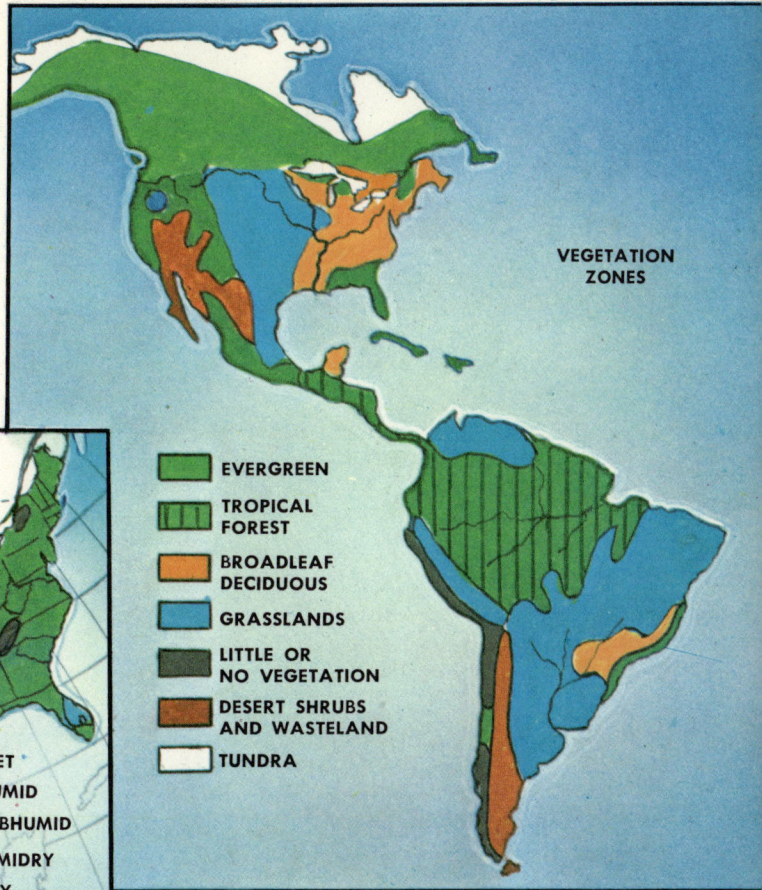

VEGETATION ZONES

EVERGREEN

TROPICAL FOREST

BROADLEAF DECIDUOUS

GRASSLANDS

LITTLE OR NO VEGETATION

DESERT SHRUBS AND WASTELAND

TUNDRA

CLIMATE ZONES

WET

HUMID

SUBHUMID

SEMIDRY

DRY

Climate as a geographical control is very important. It reaches into many aspects of human, plant, and animal life. Climate to a large extent determines the type of soil and vegetation in a given region, and because of this, influences the use of the land, whether it be for crop cultivation, forests, or grazing. Climate, in a large part, determines the ability of the land to support people and their animals. The distribution of world population reflects strongly the advantages of a favorable climate.

### FACTORS CONTROLLING CLIMATE

If temperature is used as an agent of classification of climate, one must realize that there are various factors that control or affect temperature. The higher the latitude (distance from the equator), the colder the climate. Increase in latitude also tends toward smaller daily temperature ranges but larger yearly ones.

For example, suppose a person lives within five degrees or ten degrees of the equator. Perhaps it is Panama, or the Congo, or

northern Brazil. Every day the sun shines for about 12 hours; every night is about 12 hours long. At noontime the sun is never very far from vertical, whether the month be July or January. As a result, the climate is uniformly hot throughout the year, and the average temperature is very high, perhaps about 80 degrees. There is no summer or winter. There are only rainy or dry seasons, and the average yearly range or change of temperature is only about three to four degrees.

Altitude is height above sea level. Its affect on temperature is similar to that of latitude. Increased altitude, such as in mountainous areas, means lower temperature at the average rate of three and one half degrees per 1000 feet. The higher the altitude, the lower the average yearly temperature.

Sea or land location also affect temperature ranges. Sea areas have marine climate with small changes or ranges, while land areas have continental climates with large ranges. The reason for this is that land gains or loses heat much more rapidly than water.

**Much of the strength of wind, and most of its moisture, is lost as it passes over a mountain. The side away from wind is warmer and drier**

The direction of prevailing winds has a definite affect on temperature ranges. When the winds blow from large bodies of water, temperature ranges are small; when they blow from large land areas temperature ranges are large.

Topography or structure of the land determines whether winds from distant regions affect the climate. For example, high mountain ranges often keep out winds that might otherwise affect the temperature. Southern Italy owes its balmy climate partly to the fact that cold north winds are kept out by the Alps and the Apennine Mountains.

Ocean currents may make the climate of a region warmer or colder than normal for its latitude. In one famous example, the prevailing westerlies blow from the warm Gulf Stream to the shores of Iceland, the British Isles, and Scandinavia giving these regions climate as warm as places hundreds of miles closer to the equator.

Rainfall, another way of classifying climate, is controlled by various factors. Since rainfall has a definite bearing upon climate, one should know something about these various controlling factors.

The latitude of a place determines which one or more wind belts it will be in during a year. These wind belts are of primary importance in determining the total rainfall and its seasonal occurrences.

Mountains also have a lot to do in determining rainfall. The side of a mountain that a place is located on means more or less rainfall than is normal for the area's latitude. Low rain clouds can be caught on one side.

Distance from the sea has an influence upon rainfall. Nearness to the sea, however, is no guarantee of sufficient rainfall. The desert of Peru, for example, is located next to the Pacific Ocean, yet it is one of the

**Three places quite close together may have very different climates because of variations in terrain, altitude and nearness to water. The variations show up clearly in rainfall and temperature ranges**

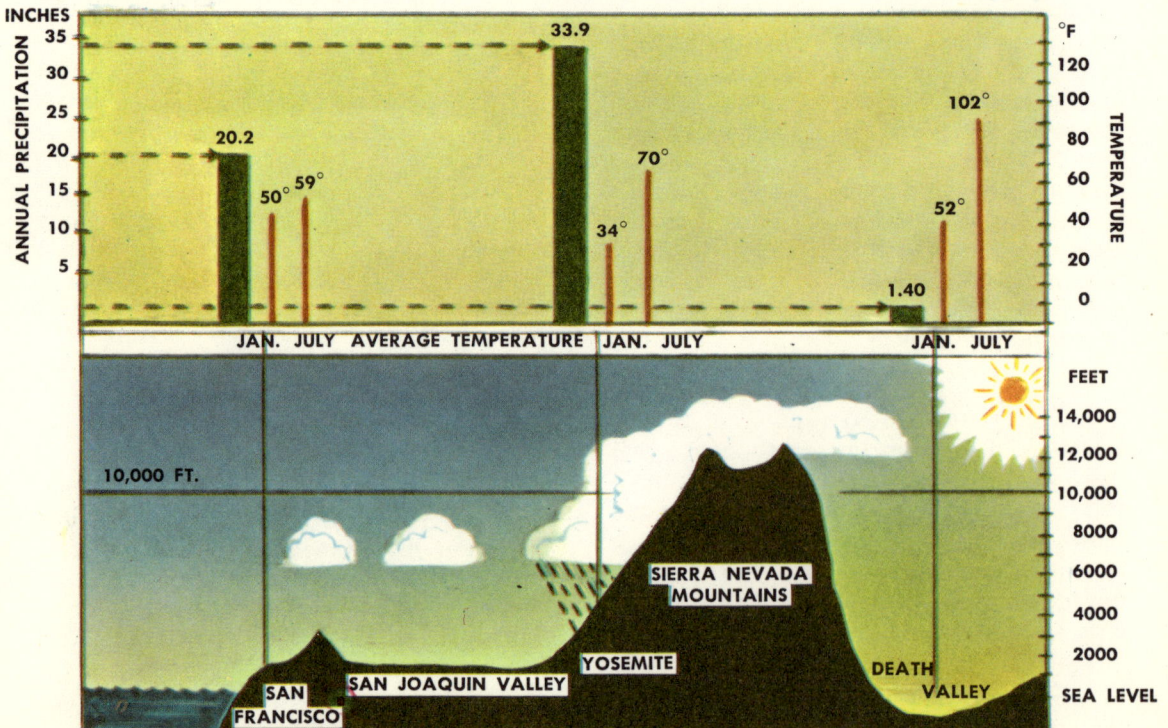

driest regions in the world. But where winds do blow from the sea, rains are likely to be heavier nearer the ocean than farther inland.

Vegetation is sometimes known as a classification of climate. Plants form an index in that certain types require special conditions of temperature and rainfall. The limits of growth of key types will give boundaries for climate zones.

One very striking illustration or example is the northern limit of tree growth. In the subarctic areas of North America and Asia, there are points beyond which trees will not grow. Another example might be the poleward limit of growth of palms, whose sensitivity to frost limits the extent of growth to about the 35 degree North or South latitude.

### CLIMATE CLASSIFICATION

There is another basic plan of classifying climate. This method was devised in 1918 by Dr. Vladimir Koppen of the University of Graz in Austria. It has become the most widely used of climatic classification for geography purposes. Each climate is defined according to fixed values of temperature and precipitation based on the average of the year or of individual months. Under this system there are five major climate groups. They are as follows:

1. *Tropical climates:* They have an average temperature for every month of above 64.4 degrees Fahrenheit. These climates have no winter season. Annual rainfall is large and exceeds the amount of evaporation.
2. *Dry climates:* Potential evaporation exceeds rainfall on the average during the year. There is no water surplus, so no permanent streams begin in these zones.
3. *Warm temperature climates:* The coldest month has an average temperature under 64.4 degrees Fahrenheit, but above 26.6 degrees. At least one month has an average temperature above 50 degrees. This climate has both summer and winter months.
4. *Snow climates:* The coldest month average temperature is under 26.6 degrees Fahrenheit. The average temperature of the warmest month is above 50 degrees.
5. *Ice climates:* An average temperature of the warmest month would be below 50 degrees Fahrenheit. This climate has no true summer.

There is also another well-known elementary school classification of climate that is still well known and widely used by many people. The classification is *Torrid* or hot zone; *Frigid* or cold zone; and two *Temperate* or in-between zones. The Tropics of Cancer and Capricorn, and the Arctic and Antarctic Circles are the boundaries.

However, this classification is not correct. Climates within these zones vary so widely that this classification is almost worthless, except for its meaning with regard to the length of daylight and the position of the sun in the sky. There are many isolated or separate cases within a zone that must be considered. For example, the deserts of the Mohave and Death Valley reach the extremes of over 120 degrees Fahrenheit, and yet they are located in the temperate zone. In the jungles of the tropical rainforest of Central America, the temperature seldom exceeds 90 degrees. It would be logical to assume that this is a rather poor way of classifying climate.

Climates are very scattered and are affected by many local and general conditions. It would be difficult to adopt entirely any one way of classifying climate.     V. V. N.

SEE ALSO: AFRICA, ASIA, AUSTRALIA, EUROPE, NORTH AMERICA, SOUTH AMERICA

**Cloaca** (klo-ACHE-uh) Cloaca is the structure in a human embryo that develops into separate canals for the rectum and bladder by the time of birth.

In birds, reptiles, amphibians and many fishes, the cloaca is the common chamber into which the intestinal, urinary and reproductive canals discharge.

The term cloaca comes from the *Cloaca Maxima* which was a great sewer in ancient Rome that drained the Forum where public debates were held.     P. G. B.

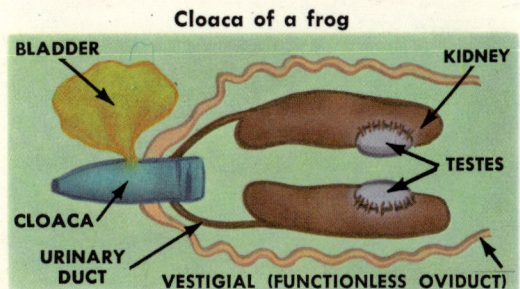

**Cloaca of a frog**

BLADDER
KIDNEY
CLOACA
TESTES
URINARY DUCT
VESTIGIAL (FUNCTIONLESS OVIDUCT)

**ALFRED B. NOBEL**
1833–1896 •
Invented dynamite,
started Nobel Prizes

**HIPPOCRATES**
460–370? B.C •
"Father of Medicine"

**MARIE CURIE**
• 1867–1934
Discovered radium
and polonium

**ENRICO FERMI**
• 1901–1954
Produced first atomic pile and first
controlled nuclear chain reaction

**THOMAS ALVA EDISON**
1847–1931 •
Invented light bulb,
phonograph and mimeograph

**NICOLAUS COPERNICUS**
• 1473–1543
First astronomer to say that Earth
goes around the sun

**LUTHER BURBANK**
• 1849–1926
Invented new
varieties of plants

**EDWARD JENNER**
1749–1823 •
Discovered smallpox vaccine

**CHARLES DARWIN**
1809-1882 •
Conceived the Theory of Evolution
through Natural Selection

**WILLIAM HARVEY**
• 1578–1657
Discovered the circulation
of the blood

**GEORGE WASHINGTON CARVER**
1864–1943 •
Experimented with
practical botany

**SAMUEL F. B. MORSE**
• 1791–1872
Invented telegraph and Morse code

**LOUIS PASTEUR**
• 1822–1895
Invented pasteurization

**BENJAMIN FRANKLIN**
• 1706–1790
Invented lightning rod